Oxford Junior

BRITAIN BECOMES A GREAT POWER

Peter & Mary Speed

Oxford University Press by arrangement with the British Broadcasting Corporation 1979

Oxford University Press, Walton Street, Oxford OX2 6DP

ISBN 0 19 918118 7

OXFORD   LONDON   GLASGOW
NEW YORK   TORONTO   MELBOURNE   WELLINGTON
KUALA LUMPUR   SINGAPORE   JAKARTA   HONG KONG   TOKYO
DELHI   BOMBAY   CALCUTTA   MADRAS   KARACHI
NAIROBI   DAR ES SALAAM   CAPE TOWN

Printed in Great Britain by Chorley and Pickersgill Ltd.
Typesetting by Tradespools Ltd., Frome, Somerset

Contents

Chapter One   The Village and the Farm

1 The Open Field Village

Let us go back to the year 1760, and visit the village of Hillidon, near Nottingham. One of the farmers, John Fowler, will be our guide.

The village stands in the middle of its fields, the farmhouses and cottages huddling round the church. John's house is no more than a living room, a kitchen and two bedrooms. He has a wife and several children, so they do not have much space. The house smells dirty, especially as there is a heap of manure in the yard.

John has a stall for his cow, a barn for his corn and hay, and a shed for his farm tools. There is no plough, and John explains that he shares one with his neighbours. They keep it in the churchyard.

'How big is your farm?' we ask. 'About ten acres.' *'Well, that won't take us long to visit.'* 'Don't you believe it. If you want to see it all you must walk several miles.'

Rather puzzled, we follow John out of the village. 'There you are,' he says, pointing to a huge field of wheat, 'there is my bread for next year.' It is August and there is a sea of ripening wheat, stretching into the distance. *'But that can't be all yours. That field is hundreds of acres!'* 'No, I just farm half an acre in Holm-side Furlong, right over there, three-quarters of an acre in Old Mill Furlong in the middle, an acre in Wilsdon Furlong to our left, and a small piece just here.' *'But how can you tell which is yours?'* John laughs. 'Oh, I know all right. And if I tried to reap a neighbour's crop, he would remind me soon enough.'

On the other side of the village we find another field, just as big as the first, but it is growing barley, peas and beans. John has the same amount of land here. Again, it is scattered in small pieces all over the field. *'You like peas and beans for dinner then, John?'* 'Not I. They are for my cow and my sheep during the winter. They have most of my barley as well, but it looks a good crop this year, and I may be able to make a drop of beer.'

We go to a third field, again as big as the others. It has no crops at all, but we can see large grass patches in the dips. They are sikes, and are where the land is too damp to plough. 'My sheep are in this field,' ex- plains John. 'They have been here since last autumn, eating the stubble and what grass they can find. They must come off soon, though, because we shall be ploughing for next year's wheat.' *'So you change the crops each year?'* 'Of course. Next year, the wheat field will grow barley, peas and beans, and the barley field will be fallow, like this one.' *'But why do you leave a field bare like this?'* 'Land needs a rest, or it is soon good for nothing.' *'But why not manure it?'* 'How should I get enough manure from one cow and six sheep?'

John now takes us to see his cow. It is another good walk, but at last we come to a long, narrow field that lies beside a stream. 'This is Stetchpool Meadow,' says John. 'I have a dole here, one a bit further along, and another at the far end.' Looking closely, we can see the field is marked out with stakes into patches no bigger than an ordinary garden. 'Of course, the meadow is really for hay,' John explains, 'but we must have all our hay cut, dried and carried by Lammas Tide. (August 1st.) We then graze our cows on the

ploughs

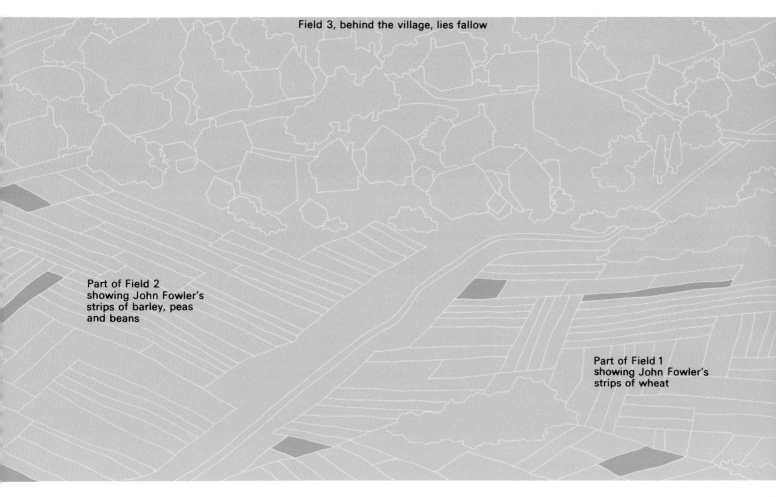

Field 3, behind the village, lies fallow

Part of Field 2
showing John Fowler's
strips of barley, peas
and beans

Part of Field 1
showing John Fowler's
strips of wheat

aftermath. That is the grass which grows after we have cut our hay. Soon, we shall cut our wheat, and when it is all in, the sexton will ring the church bell, and we shall put our cows in that field for a time. We have to shift them around to graze where they can. I'm lucky because I have a bit of land. My animals can go all over the fallow field and the meadow. Villagers with no land have to put their beasts on the common. Grass doesn't grow in the winter, so they go hungry.'

He breaks off to point to a small, lean animal. 'There's my cow. She is happy enough now, but she won't be tomorrow. It's my turn for the plough, and she will have to help pull it.'

'Who sees you obey all the rules in your village, John?' 'The manor court, of course. We all belong to it, and take office in turn. I am a burlyman this year. There are four of us and we keep an eye on the fields. We see no-one ploughs the sikes, or anyone else's land. If they do, we tell the court and they fine them. They fined me last year because I didn't clean out my ditches.'

'Where do you sell your meat, John?' 'I don't sell meat, unless an animal drops dead. Dead animals are no good to me.' *'What about your crops, then?'*

'You must be daft. When the animals have eaten all they want, there is precious little left for the wife and children, let alone to sell. You must talk to Jack Hayward. He farms eighty acres and he has plenty to sell. He takes it to Nottingham, I think. I don't know. I never leave the village.'

2 Enclosing the Village

Today we will pay another visit to Hillidon. From the ale house we can hear the men arguing and banging on the furniture. Obviously something important has happened since we were last here. The squire, the parson and some of the richer farmers have persuaded Parliament to pass an Enclosure Act for Hillidon. Everyone will have to give up his land, and then it will all be shared out again. This time each farmer will have his land in one piece, instead of little bits scattered everywhere. He will have a number of fields, like those we have today, and he will have to plant hedges round them. In other words, he will have to 'enclose' his farm.

Three gentlemen called Enclosure Commissioners have arrived in the village. They have asked everyone how much land they think they should have, and have put up a list of the claims in the church. That, as much as anything, is what is causing the excitement.

John Fowler was puzzled. He knew he had ten acres of land, but that was not all. He also had the right to graze his animals all over the fallow field and the meadow. If he could not keep his animals, he would be ruined, so he asked for another five acres. 'Five acres to feed those beasts of yours?' says one of the villagers. 'Your cow is all skin and bone, she gives you no more than a couple of pints of milk a day in summer, and is dry all winter. Your sheep have backs like rabbits, and between them they don't give enough wool to make a waistcoat.'

'You aren't one to talk, Bill Finch,' replies John. 'You have no land at all. You only keep a couple of pigs and some geese on the common, but you are asking for three acres of land.'   'Yes, Bill Finch,' says another man, 'and you have no right to use the common anyway. We only let you to keep you off the parish.'   'Rubbish,' says Bill. 'I have always used the common, so did my father, and his father before him.'   'Lies,' says John. 'I shall tell the Commissioners you

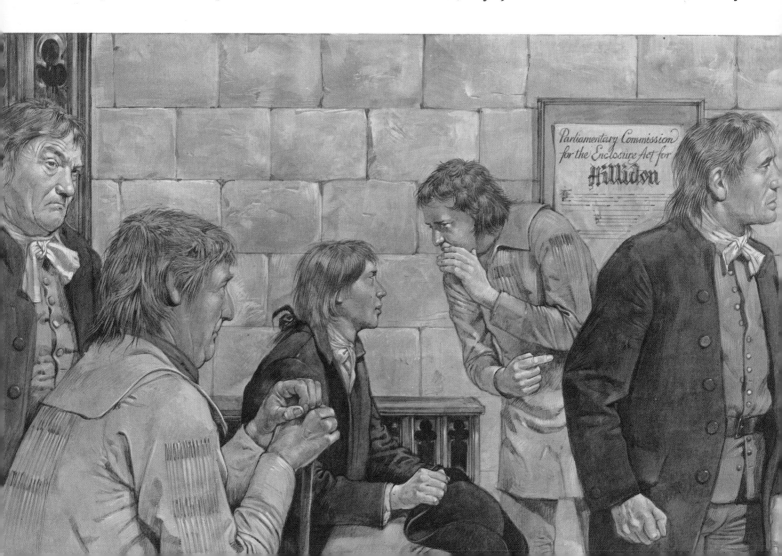

are a liar, and you will have no land at all.'

Just then someone else comes into the room. He is much better dressed than the others. They all turn on him. 'It's a wonder you dare show your face here, Hayward,' someone shouts. 'You and the Squire have had this Act and it will ruin us all.' 'I don't think so,' Hayward replies. 'I am tired of being bossed by the manor court, and I am tired of having to farm like you.' 'What's wrong with our farming?' 'There's plenty wrong with your sheep for a start. Some of mine died of liver rot they caught from yours. And I have been telling you for years we should grow turnips and clover on the fallow field.' 'Who wants to poison their sheep with turnips or wear out their soil with clover?' 'A crop of clover does the soil good,' Hayward replies. At this, the villagers all roar with laughter. 'Well,' says Hayward, 'soon I shall be able to farm in my own way. Then you will see.'

The Enclosure Commissioners met the villagers one by one. John was worried because he had no papers at all to prove his farm really did belong to him. Luckily some of his friends were ready to swear he had always used the land and that no-one had ever challenged him. The Commissioners looked doubtful and

John was left for months wondering what would happen.

After nearly two years the Commissioners finished their work, and gave the parson their Award. It was forty sheets of parchment, each three feet by two feet. It said exactly who was to have every scrap of land in the village. The squire had the most with well over a thousand acres. The parson had about four hundred. Three of the wealthy villagers had two hundred acres each. Hayward had seventy acres. The poorest villagers who had kept beasts on the common were given half an acre each. No-one could feed a cow on that.

John only had eight acres. They were in one block of land, which was convenient, but they were part of the old common and were over a mile from the village. He had two years to enclose his land, that is, to plant a hedge round it. The hedge would give him a lot of work and expense, but worse was to follow. There was also a bill. Parliament charged £2,000 for the Enclosure Act, and the Commissioners charged £3,000 for their work. Everyone with land had to help pay. John's share was over £30, which was more money than he had ever seen in his life. How was he to find it? He was beside himself with worry.

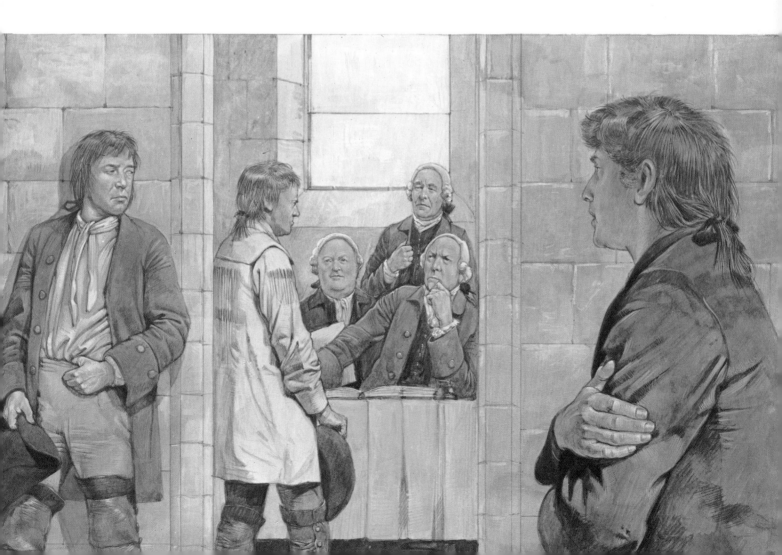

Enclosing the Village

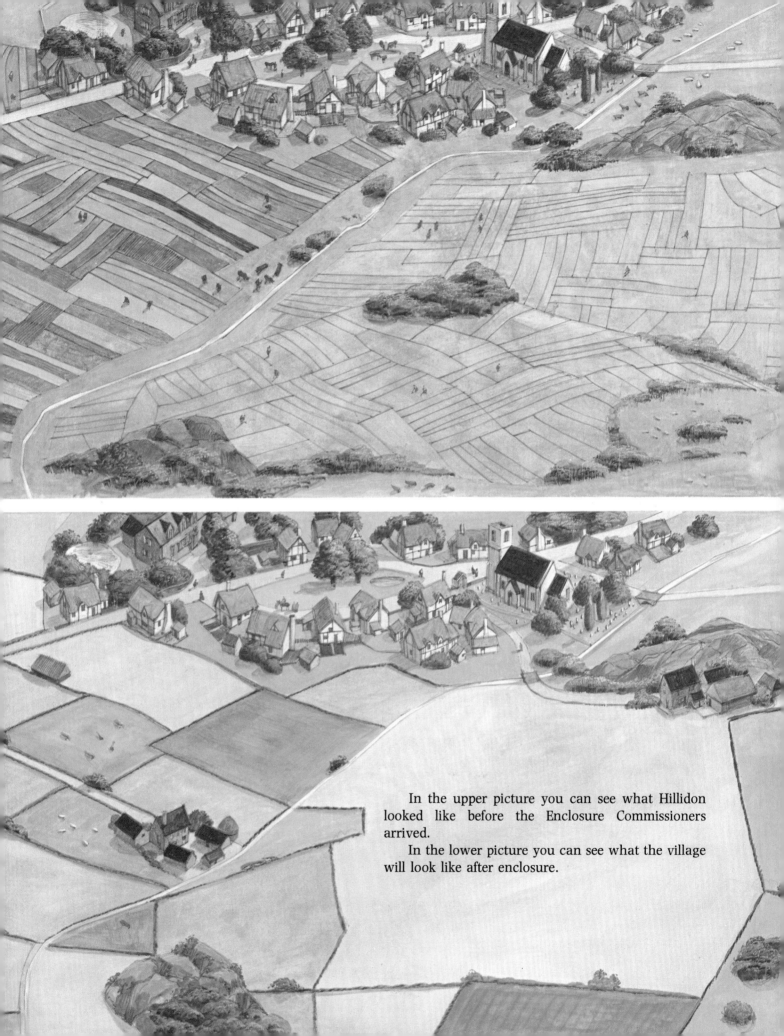

In the upper picture you can see what Hillidon looked like before the Enclosure Commissioners arrived.

In the lower picture you can see what the village will look like after enclosure.

3 New Ways of Farming

Why was it that people like Hayward wanted to enclose their land?

For a long time the towns had been growing, and their people wanted to buy food. Farmers like John Fowler grew only enough for themselves, but men with more land had food for sale. They made so much money from it that they wanted to grow more and still more. They knew, too, that there were ways they could do this from the same amount of land.

Back in the 1560s, during the reign of Elizabeth I, some Dutch people fled from a terrible war in their own country and settled in Norfolk. Soon the Norfolk people were amazed at some strange plants the Dutchmen were growing in their gardens. They were turnips. Cautiously, the English tried them and soon they, too, were growing them in their gardens. Then someone, we do not know who, grew them in a field as winter feed for his sheep. Other farmers copied him, and within a hundred years turnips were a common crop in East Anglia. During the winter, grass does not grow, and a farmer may be short of hay. If he has turnips, though, he can give his animals something to eat.

The Dutch also brought new kinds of clover, much better than the wild sort found in England. Hayward was quite right about clover: it does do the soil good. Also, if clover and grass are sown together, they give heavy crops of hay.

After a time, farmers in Norfolk realised they could manage without fallow, and plant all their land if they grew the new crops in rotation with the old. They sowed a field with wheat in the first year, turnips in the second, barley, beans or peas in the third, and grasses with clover in the fourth. Usually, they let the grasses and clover stay for a few years before going back to wheat. We call this the 'Norfolk Four Course' system. A nobleman called Viscount Townshend was so keen on it, they called him 'Turnip Townshend'.

You will remember that John Fowler did not want to plant the fallow field because he did not have enough manure. Farmers who grew the new crops, though, had turnips and a lot more hay, so they kept more animals. The animals gave plenty of manure. The crops fed the animals, the animals manured the crops, and the farmers made a lot of money.

Also, there were new breeds of animal. A man called Robert Bakewell, of Dishley in Leicestershire, bred sheep which fattened so quickly that they were ready for the butcher in two years. Two brothers called Colling from County Durham bred some new cattle called shorthorns, which gave plenty of milk and meat. John Fowler's sheep would never have grown fat. He had them for wool and for dung. His cow was a poor little thing that he kept until she dropped dead from hard work.

the Norfolk four course system

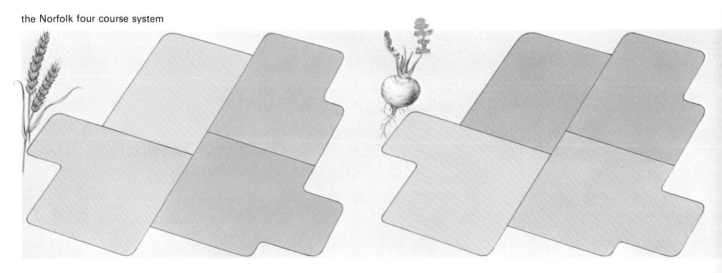

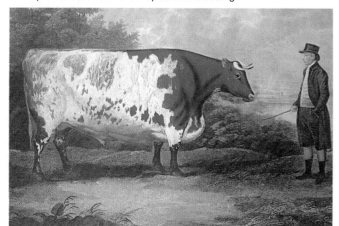

this Durham shorthorn and the Leicester sheep are examples of the improved stock achieved by careful breeding.

We can now see Hayward's problem. He wanted to try new crops, but if he planted turnips on his part of the fallow field, John Fowler's sheep would eat them. Also, he wanted to try the Norfolk system, but it needed four, five, six, or even more fields. That was impossible at Hillidon, while Fowler and his friends insisted on having three fields.

Moreover, Hayward dared not buy expensive Leicestershire sheep and shorthorn cows. If he did, they would have to mix with animals belonging to the other villagers, and would catch diseases from them.

What Hayward wanted was to have his land all in one piece, fenced off from everyone else's. Only then could he grow the crops he wanted and keep the best animals. Unlike his neighbours he had travelled a bit, and had spoken to owners of enclosed farms. Some with no more land than he had were making twice as much money. He wanted to do the same.

4 The Squire

the old Squire builds his house

The Squire

We will now go forward seventy years and visit Hillidon in 1830. This time we will call on the squire, Sir William Courteney. He is a rich man, being squire of several villages, apart from Hillidon. His father had lived in a Tudor mansion. It was picturesque, but it was cold and draughty. He pulled it down and began an elegant new house. His son has just finished it.

Sir William is too busy to see us for the moment, but his agent, Mr. Starkes, meets us very politely. We ask him what work an agent does. 'I look after Sir William's estates. The most important thing I do is collect his rents, but that only takes a week or two at Michaelmas. I have to manage the home farm, which supplies the family and all the servants in the big house. We have an excellent herd of Jersey cows, so we are never short of milk, cream and butter. Then we have a brick works, a timber yard, a saw mill and a forge, all belonging to the estate. I have to keep an eye on them. If farm buildings need mending, the tenant has to do the work, but Sir William gives him the bricks and timber for nothing. It is my job to see them delivered. At the forge we mend the farm machines and make things like gate hinges, horse shoes and nails.

'My most difficult job, though, is to make sure the tenants take proper care of their farms. You see, each one has a lease, which is an agreement he has made with Sir William. Sir William promises the tenant he can keep his farm for twenty-one years, and a man could ruin it in that time. So that he does not, he must agree to grow his crops in the right way. We usually make tenants follow the Norfolk system – wheat, turnips, barley and then grasses for a year or two. We never let them take two straw crops one after the other. During the war, wheat was so dear they would have sown it on every inch of land. That would have ruined it, so we made them stick to the proper course. They grumbled at the time, but it paid off. The land is still in good heart.'

The big open fields, meadows and common have all gone, and in their place is a patchwork of smaller fields, just like today. There is no fallow land, but crops everywhere. The cows and sheep look much fatter than they did before, and we pass one or two farmers who look as fat and contented as their animals. There are, though, a lot of poor people in the village. Some of them are men who are out of work.

14

'This village grows a lot of food, Mr. Starkes.' 'Yes, since the Enclosure Act, everything has about doubled – crops, livestock and, I am pleased to say, Sir William's rents. He finds ways of spending the money, though. He has more debts than his father, and that is saying something. He can't resist buying land. Whenever there is a bit for sale, he snaps it up, whether he can afford it or not. The biggest worry, though, is the expense at the big house, with all those servants and all those parties.'

We return to the big house, passing through the huge iron gates into the park. Other guests are coming back from hunting, excited and happy. At the house we change into our best clothes and, when the gong sounds, go down to dinner. The house has a marble staircase, paintings on the walls and expensive furniture in all the rooms. In the dining hall the mahogany tables and sideboards are set with dishes of gold and silver. An orchestra plays in a gallery. There are servants dressed in livery everywhere.

The dinner is a dozen courses, with all the wine we can drink – too much in fact. At eleven o'clock the meal is over and the ladies go to the drawing room.

The men stay, drinking. They become noisy, telling rude stories and making unkind jokes. After a couple of hours they become bored and join the ladies. Groups of people play cards while others stand around gossiping. Towards two o'clock people begin to leave and we, too, stagger to our beds.

In the morning we wake up feeling dreadful. However can we make polite conversation? There is no need to worry. Sir William keeps out of the way, and none of the other guests wants to talk. Breakfast is set in the dining room, and we just help ourselves.

It is now time to say goodbye. We find Sir William in the estate office having a heated argument with Mr. Starkes, obviously about money. He breaks off, though, to wish us a kindly farewell, and says he hopes we will come and see him again before long.

5 Farmers

One of the best farms in the village belongs to George Hayward. He is the grandson of Jack Hayward, who was alive at the time of the Enclosure Act.

His farm is well away from the village. There is a large, square house, and a yard with fine, solid buildings round it. The largest is the great barn with two sets of double doors, big enough for a waggon. It has a threshing floor in the middle, though this is no longer used. Then there are the cow stalls, stables, cart sheds, pig sties, poultry houses and dog kennels. One building has a water wheel and inside is a powerful threshing machine. Everywhere there are animals – horses, cows, oxen, sheep, pigs, one or two goats, a donkey, hens, geese, ducks, turkeys, pigeons and even peacocks. Behind the house is a flower garden with beehives.

The Haywards have expensive furniture. There is a table and a sideboard of mahogany, comfortable armchairs, carpets and curtains. Mr. Hayward is proud of the silver cups his animals have won at cattle shows, and his wife is nearly as proud of her gooseberry wine, her home-made cakes, and her embroidery.

'You are a rich man, Mr. Hayward,' we say. 'I do well enough, but I owe most of it to my grandfather. You see, he fought hard to have the Enclosure Act for this village, even though it made him unpopular. The Commissioners awarded him seventy acres, and he expected to make a good living from that. Then along comes Sir William, the father of the one we have now. "Jack," he says, "I will give you £30 an acre for your land." "Fine, squire," says grandfather, "but how does a farmer live without land?" "Don't you worry," says Sir William. "I shall soon have some farms ready of about 200 acres, each with its hedges planted, and with a new house and buildings. You shall have one of them if you want. I will give you a long lease and charge only £1 an acre rent for the year. Think of it Jack – a farm of 200 acres and over £2,000 in your pocket." My grandfather saw the squire was right, so they did the deal. The farm has done well ever since, especially during the war.'

'But you are only tenants now. Sir William could turn you out, if he wanted.' 'Not until my lease is up he can't. Even then he will give me a new one. Sir William never gets rid of a good tenant. We will just have to agree a new rent, that is all.'

'Sir William is a fair man?' 'Very fair. Back in 1823 when we could hardly sell our wheat he let me off most of my rent. I don't like Starkes though. He caught me selling a load of dung the other day – just a load of dung, but he stopped me and said he would fine me £5 if I did it again.'

Mr. Hayward takes us to see his water meadows. They are by a stream and from time to time he floods them. His grandfather had one crop of hay from his meadow, and grazed animals there for six weeks. George has three crops of hay and twelve weeks grazing. This is because the water helps the grass to grow. George is especially pleased since he wants to keep more animals and grow less wheat. 'During the war,' he explains, 'we had very good prices for wheat so we grew all we could – that is all Starkes would let us. Now wheat gets cheaper the whole time. Meat, butter and cheese hold their price, though, so I keep more sheep and cows.' *Do you grow turnips for winter feed?* 'Not the old kind. They couldn't stand the frost and rotted in the ground after Christmas. I have Swedish turnips now, and they last until the water meadows are ready for their first bite at the end of February. My animals grow fat, and my cows give milk all through the winter. Before enclosure my grandfather was lucky if he just kept his stock alive. I still go on making my farm better, like when I first tried swedes, and when I bought my threshing machine. Before enclosure no-one could change his farming like I do. The small farmers ate all they grew, so they didn't bother about prices. They never wanted change and they held back the better men. Things are different now, thank goodness.'

'But what happened to the small farmers after enclosure, Mr. Hayward?' 'You go into the village, and you will see.'

6 Farm Labourers

Back in the village there are a lot more people than there were in 1760. Most of the men are farm labourers, and among them is James Fowler, grandson of John Fowler. He lives in the same house, though he shares it with another family. It never was pleasant but now it is a dirty slum, with its walls crumbling and its thatch leaking. James Fowler has a sad story to tell.

'After the Enclosure Act, my grandfather was given eight acres of land. It was a mile from home, which didn't please him, and he had to plant a hedge round it, which pleased him less. His big worry, though, was the £30 bill he had for enclosure expenses. He asked the parson what to do about it, and the parson sent him to a lawyer in town. That man was as sharp as they come. He said he would give grandfather a mortgage of £30 on his land, and grandfather had to promise to pay him £5 a year for eight years. Grandfather thought that was hardly fair, but he had no choice. Anyway, he paid his £30 bill with the money the lawyer gave him. His troubles were just beginning, though. He had some land, but he had lost his common rights. In the old days, his animals had wandered all over the fallow field and the meadow. Now the land had been divided and fenced. He needed his eight acres to grow food for his family, so he sold his animals. He was much poorer and he could see it was going to be a struggle to pay his mortgage. Then one day the squire sent for him. "John," he said, "I will give you £25 an acre for your land." My grandfather was overjoyed. He saw he could pay his debts easily and have what looked like a fortune in ready money. He should have wondered what he was going to do when all the money was spent, but he never thought of that. Anyway, he bought himself and his wife new clothes, stood everyone drinks at the "Three Horseshoes" for a few nights and then went to pay the lawyer his £30. That man told grandfather he would be wise to put the rest of his money into Allen's Bank, which was what he did. The bank paid a bit of interest on the money for a few years, and then it went broke. Grandfather lost everything.' *'How did he make a living?'* 'He went labouring, of course. The Fowlers were yeoman farmers for generations. Since the enclosures they have been day labourers. It is all the fault of the enclosures.'

Other men in the village are just as unhappy. Dick Finch said that his ancestors had always been labourers, but in the old days life had been different. 'Most of them kept a pig or a couple of sheep on the common and their wives spun thread. Now the common is gone, and the beasts with it. All the spinning is done in factories these days, so the only time our women can earn a few pennies is during the harvest. As for the single men, they used to live in with the farmers. That meant they slept under a sound roof and ate good food. Nowadays, Hayward and his kind have bought fancy furniture and carpets. They don't want us in with them. We wear muddy boots and smell of dung. The worst thing lately has been the threshing machines. Not so long ago, four of us used to spend all winter in Hayward's barn, threshing out his wheat. It was hard, dull work, mind, but it gave us a wage through the winter. Now his machine finishes the work in a week. He turns us away then, and tells us not to come back until spring.'

Dick's wife tells us about her housekeeping. They are seven in the family, husband, wife and five children. She spends nine shillings a week on bread, a shilling a week on meat and cheese, and has to find sixpence a week rent. Nearly every year she either has a baby, or one of the children dies, so births and burials cost the family over £1 a year, or about sixpence a week. Candles, soap and a few other things come to a shilling. All together, then, they have to find twelve shillings a week, even if they spend nothing on clothes. Dick's wages are only nine shillings a week, when he has work.

'However do you manage, Mrs. Finch?' 'We go on the parish. A miserable life that is, too. We don't starve, but we come so close to it that at times it were better to be dead.'

7 The Poor

the overseers

Matthew Ramsden is one of the overseers of the poor at Hillidon. *'How did you become an overseer, Mr. Ramsden?'* 'I was elected. Every year those of us that pay rates, the farmers, the innkeeper and so on, meet in the church vestry. We choose the parish officers from among ourselves. It was Hayward's idea that I should be overseer. He doesn't like me. Still, I had my own back and named him as constable. Many a night he has had to come into the village to stop a fight at the "Three Horseshoes". It's less trouble than being overseer, mind. That takes me away from my farm a lot.' *'How much are you paid?'* 'Why, nothing, of course. The one comfort is, I can give up the job at the end of the year. I will try and see Hayward gets it.'

'What do you have to do?' 'Well, when I first took office, I sat down with the other overseer, Luke Chambers, and we tried to decide how much money we were going to need during the year. We looked at last year's expenses, and did a bit of guess work. Then we worked out how much each of the ratepayers owed, and went and told them. You can imagine how popular that made us. Poor rates this year were 15/– an acre, which is getting on for as much as we pay in rent. A man like Hayward can afford to pay, but others like Luke and me can barely keep our own families decently. It comes hard to give more than we can afford to keep a lot of paupers in idleness.'

'What do you do with the money?' 'We give it out to the paupers. They come along with their wives, all dressed in rags, and with their snivelling brats, and tell us how they suffer. Luke and I know there are several men who could work if they wanted.' *'Why not refuse to pay them?'* 'I don't want my ricks fired do I?' *'How do you decide what they should have?'* 'The Justices of the Peace, that's Sir William Courteney and his fine friends, say we must use the allowance system. Every family must have enough bread to eat, and if they don't have the money to buy it, the parish must give it to them. Say they need nine shillings for bread, and they only have seven shillings, well, the parish must pay them two shillings.' *'That way no-one need starve.'* 'True, but it runs away with the money. Take a man like Finch. His wife has a baby nearly every year, but he doesn't worry, because he knows the parish will feed them. He doesn't work, either, no more than two or three days in the week. He knows that if he hasn't enough money, the parish must find it for him. Men like Hayward do well out of it, too. Hayward stands off most of his men in the winter, and the parish has to keep them. When they are in work, he only gives them eight or nine shillings

a parish notice-board

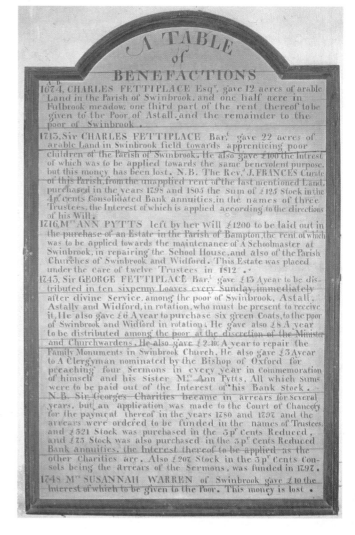

a week. They went to him the other day and asked for a rise. All he said was, "If your wages aren't high enough, the parish will make them up." It's people like Luke and me that suffer. We employ no labour, so we can't tell our men to live off the parish. Really, we are paying most of Hayward's wages for him.'

'*When we spoke to the poor, they blamed the enclosures. They said they would be all right if they could have their common back and keep a cow, or a pig or two.*' 'That's rubbish. The enclosed farms need much more labour than the old ones. Remember, there was no work done on the fallow field for a whole year, apart from ploughing it a couple of times. Now all the land is cultivated. No, the trouble is that we have too many labourers in Hillidon. The farmers can't employ them all.' '*Why don't some of them move?*' 'Sir William helped a few families to emigrate, and two or three more have gone into Nottingham. Only the best ones go, though. Men like Finch haven't the spirit. He and his kind are going to ruin Luke and me.'

Help was, in fact, on its way for Matthew and Luke. In 1834 Parliament passed an Act which changed the whole system of looking after the poor. Hillidon joined with fifteen other parishes to make a Poor Law Union. All the ratepayers elected a Board of Guardians, of twenty men. Matthew was one of them, but apart from four meetings a year, he had nothing to do. The Union was rich enough to pay full-time officers for the day-to-day work. In 1840, they opened a workhouse, and stopped giving the paupers money. If anyone was starving he could either go into the workhouse or stay hungry. Dick Finch tried it. He found he had to get up early in the morning, wear a uniform and live on plain food, like bread and watery porridge. He had no beer and no tobacco. His wife and children were taken from him and put in another part of the workhouse. What was worst, though, he had to spend the entire day smashing bones with a hammer. He soon decided it would be better to find a job.

Mrs. Fowler was unlucky. Her husband died and she had to go to the workhouse with her children. Most of the people there were widows and orphans. They had a miserable time.

Work Section

Understand Your Work

1 The Open Field Village
1 Draw a plan of John Fowler's house and farm yard.
2 Make a list of the crops John Fowler grows. What does he do with each?
3 What animals does John Fowler keep? What use are they to him?
4 Where do John Fowler's animals graze?
5 What is the work of the manor court?
6 How is Jack Hayward different from John Fowler?
7 Describe the use of a) the open fields b) the common c) the meadow.
8 How many open fields are there? What is growing on each?
9 What is meant by leaving a field 'fallow'?
10 Why is it done?

2 Enclosing the Village
1 How will enclosing the village change the farms?
2 Which people want the village to be enclosed?
3 What is the work of the Enclosure Commissioners?
4 How much land did John Fowler claim? Why? Why was he worried when he met the Enclosure Commissioners?
5 How much land does Bill Finch want? Why do the other villagers object?
6 What changes did Jack Hayward wish to see?
7 What is an Enclosure Award?
8 Say how the land of the village was shared.
9 How much land would Bill Finch have had?
10 How much land did John Fowler have? Why was he worried?

3 New Ways of Farming
1 Why did men with large farms want to grow more food?
2 From which country did turnips come?
3 Why were they first grown in England?
4 Why did farmers find them useful?
5 Name another new crop that was grown.
6 What was the 'Norfolk Four Course' system? Which nobleman was interested in it?
7 Why did farmers who grew the new crops have plenty of manure? How did it help them?
8 Who produced a) a new breed of sheep b) a new breed of cattle?
9 How were these new animals different from John Fowler's?
10 Why was Jack Hayward unable to grow the new crops and keep the new breeds of animal? What would make it possible for him to do so?

4 The Squire
1 Make a list of the duties of a land agent.
2 Which of these duties does Starkes say is the most important? Which is most difficult?
3 How has the village changed since enclosure?
4 What is a lease?
5 What promise does a landlord make in a lease?

6 What promises must a tenant make in return?
7 What might tempt a tenant to break his promises?
8 How did the Enclosure Act help the squire?
9 How does the squire spend his money?
10 How does the squire entertain his guests?

5 Farmers
1 Draw a plan of George Hayward's farm yard and buildings.
2 What animals does he keep?
3 Say what it is like inside the Haywards' house.
4 What bargain did the squire offer George Hayward's grandfather, Jack? Why did Jack accept?
5 In what ways does a good landlord look after his tenants?
6 Why do you suppose Starkes stopped George from selling dung?
7 What are water meadows?
8 How are they better than ordinary meadows?
9 What changes has George Hayward made on his farm?
10 Why does he say he is luckier than his grandfather was, before enclosure?

6 Farm Labourers
1 How did John Fowler find the money to pay his enclosure expenses?
2 Why did he sell his animals?
3 Why did he sell his farm?
4 What happened to his money?
5 What became of him in the end?
6 According to Dick Finch, why were labourers better off before enclosure?
7 Why can labourers' wives no longer make money by spinning?
8 Where had unmarried labourers once lived? Why do they no longer?
9 Why does Dick Finch hate threshing machines?
10 Make a list of Mrs. Finch's expenses.

7 The Poor
1 How did Matthew Ramsden become overseer of the poor? Why does he not want the job?
2 Who has to pay money to the overseers of the poor? What do the overseers do with the money?
3 What is the 'allowance system'?
4 Why does the allowance system please some of the poor?
5 Why do rich farmers like the allowance system?
6 Who dislikes the allowance system? Why?
7 What do poor people blame for all their troubles?
8 How does Matthew Ramsden explain all the poverty in Hillidon?
9 How was the system of looking after the poor changed in 1834?
10 What happened to Dick Finch and Mrs. Fowler?

Use Your Imagination

The figures in brackets tell you which section will help you answer the question.

1 Write a list of rules a manor court might draw up. (1)
2 Imagine you are John Fowler's cow. Say where you graze at different times of the year, and what other food you have. What use are you to your master? (1, 2)
3 John Fowler, Bill Finch and Jack Hayward go home and tell their wives what happened at the ale house. Write what each one says. (2)
4 You are an Enclosure Commissioner. Write your diary for the days when you:
    a first arrived in Hillidon.
    b interviewed John Fowler.
    c made your Award. (2)
5 You are a rich farmer in Hillidon and you want the village enclosed. You call a meeting to persuade the other farmers to agree. Write your speech. (3)
6 You are Mr. Starkes. Draw up a lease for a tenant of one of Sir William Courteney's farms. (4, 5)
7 Imagine you are Sir William Courteney. Describe the life you lead. How do you treat your tenants? (4, 5)
8 You have visited George Hayward's farm. Write a report on it for Sir William Courteney. (5)
9 If George Hayward could visit Hillidon today, what differences would he notice? What would he find much the same? (5)
10 A rich farmer and a poor labourer argue about enclosures. Write what they say. (6)
11 What do you think Sir William Courteney might have done to help the poor people of Hillidon? (6, 7)
12 Write a report for a newspaper on the problem of poverty before 1834. Include:
    a Overseers of the poor.
    b The allowance system.
    c Causes of poverty.
    d Suffering of the poor. (7)
13 You are Matthew Ramsden. Write a letter to a friend to convince him that the changes made after 1834 were good. (7)
14 Write a short story, based on the history of the Fowler family. (All)
15 What do you think were a) the advantages b) the disadvantages of enclosing a village? (All)

Further Work

1 Make a list of local place names which remind you of farming in the old days.
2 Find pictures of old farm tools and machinery.
3 Look through art books and find pictures of people and places, like the ones mentioned in this section.
4 Look in your local museum for farm tools, utensils and furniture belonging to the eighteenth and early nineteenth centuries.
5 If you live in the country, find out what crops the local farmers grow, and what breeds of cattle they keep.
6 Find out more about workhouses. For example, read Dickens's description of workhouse life in *Oliver Twist*, Chapters One and Two.

Chapter Two   Famous Inventors

1 John Kay and James Hargreaves

It is the year 1780. Today we will visit a village in Lancashire where they make cotton cloth. It is no use asking the way to the factory, for there is none. Instead, people are working in their own homes. From some of the cottages we can hear a strange rattle – latitat, latitat, latitat. We go into one of these houses, which belongs to William Hobbs. It is small, but it is warm and comfortable, with good oak furniture. There is a dresser, with some expensive china, there is a clock on the wall, and a couple of pictures. This is not the home of a poor man.

The weaver is busy with his loom, which is making the 'latitat' noise. William explains how it works, but it is rather complicated. 'Well, I will try and make it easy for you. First of all, I put the warp threads in the loom. They are the ones that run the whole length of the cloth. Next, I weave in the weft. This thread runs from side to side. First I wind it on a bobbin. Then I put the bobbin in my shuttle and that carries the weft left, right, left, right, from one side of the loom to the other. I use a flying shuttle, of course.'   *'What is a flying shuttle?'*   'It is one that runs on wheels. I tap it from side to side by jerking this wooden peg. Otherwise, I would have to pass the shuttle through by hand.'

This flying shuttle was invented by a weaver called John Kay in 1733. It could be fitted to any loom, and was quite cheap. It did make a big difference, though, because a man could weave twice as quickly as before. Kay was pleased with his invention, and showed it to his neighbours. To his dismay, they were furious. They said that if one weaver could do the work of two, half of them would be unemployed. They were so cruel to Kay that he fled to France, where he died soon afterwards, poor and miserable. There came a time, though, when the weavers were able to sell all the cloth they could make. They were quick enough to use the flying shuttle then, and many, like William Hobbs, made a good living because of it.

'The flying shuttle did give us problems, though,' says William. 'When we first had it, we used up the yarn so fast that the spinners could not keep us supplied. They only had the old-fashioned wheels that spun one thread at a time. We used to bribe them with presents to work hard, but they couldn't keep up with us. Not that they tried very much. They had the advantage over us and gave themselves airs and graces, as well as charging dear for their work. It's

a flying shuttle

the spinning jenny

luckier than Kay, though. His mill did quite well and he earned enough to be comfortable, though he never became rich.

better now. They all have spinning jennies. The thread isn't a lot of good. It's uneven and soft, so we can only use it for weft. Still, there is plenty of it.'

William now leaves his loom. 'That's enough weaving for today. I have done four hours. Now I am going up to the Rose and Crown for a drink with my friends. This afternoon I expect I will do a bit of gardening, and I shall have to milk my cow.'

Next door, we find Jane Hudson busy with her spinning jenny. 'This is a fine machine,' she explains. 'It is a new one, that spins sixty threads at once. Some of the old kind only spun eight threads. Still, even that was a great advance on the one thread wheel. The only problem is, that we spin too much yarn. The weavers can't use it all. Mr. Hookham, our employer, pays them more and more, but all they do then, is to work less and less. Look at Hobbs. He's finished for the day already.'

The spinning jenny was invented by a Blackburn man, James Hargreaves. On the old-fashioned wheel, the piece that twisted the thread was the spindle. It stuck out sideways. One day, Hargreaves's wife knocked her wheel over, so that the spindle was upright, but still turning round. Hargreaves at once thought, 'Why not put several spindles in a frame, and spin a number of threads at once?' It took him three years to perfect his machine, but he finished in the end. He then offered some models for sale. Instead of eager customers, though, a crowd of angry spinners invaded his home, and smashed all his machines. They were afraid of losing their jobs. Hargreaves fled to Nottingham, where he opened a spinning mill, using his jennies. Unfortunately he could not afford to take out a patent on his machine, so other men copied it, making a lot of money for themselves. Hargreaves was

2 Richard Arkwright

As we have seen, William Hobbs had his weft from housewives who worked with spinning jennies. He also needed warp. As warp threads run the whole length of the cloth, they have to be firm and strong. To see where they came from, we have to go into the Peak District, to the village of Cromford.

Cromford lies in the beautiful valley of the River Derwent. There are wooded hills all round, and trees overhang the water. In the village we find the usual things – a church, a public house, and rows of cottages. All the buildings, though, are new. The houses are clean and well built. They are in neat rows with lawns in front of them, and allotments behind. The cobbled street is shaded with trees. Almost everyone here works in the mill, a splendid building, with a huge water wheel. The whole village belongs to Richard Arkwright.

Arkwright was born in Preston in 1732. He came from a poor family, but he wanted to be rich. He was always saying 'One day I will ride in my carriage.' That is like saying, today, 'I will own a Rolls-Royce.' When he grew up, Arkwright became a barber, but he knew he could not make a fortune that way. Preston was a cotton town, so he decided to invent a spinning machine.

Many years before, a man called Lewis Paul had tried spinning with rollers. In spinning, you must not only twist the thread, but stretch it. Lewis Paul did so by passing it through two pairs of rollers, one pair going faster than the other. His machine had failed, but Arkwright thought he could succeed. He was not a craftsman, so he asked a carpenter and a clockmaker to help him. Soon, he could think of nothing but his machine. Sometimes, when he was shaving a customer, he had an idea. He then rushed off to his workshop, leaving the man sitting in the chair: one half of his face was shaved, and the other half was still covered with soap.

Mrs. Arkwright was worried. She thought her husband was going to lose all his customers, so one day she burnt his machine. Arkwright was furious. 'How much housekeeping money do I give you?' he shouted. 'Five shillings a week,' she answered. 'I promise you,' he said, 'that you will always have your

Cromford mill

five shillings a week. You will never starve.'

As we have seen, Lancashire people hated spinning machines, so, like Hargreaves, Arkwright moved to Nottingham. Here he was lucky. He met two rich stocking manufacturers, Jedediah Strutt and Samuel Need. They were already producing woollen and silk stockings, and wanted to make cotton ones as well. No-one, though, could spin cotton thread that was good enough. However, it looked as if Arkwright might, so they made him a partner in their firm. The machine was still far from perfect, and as time went by, Need grew impatient. He used to stump about, holding up some of Arkwright's thread, saying, 'Fine stuff this, to make a man ride in his carriage, all bumps and burs: fine stuff this.' Arkwright was not discouraged. Again he found a carpenter to help him. They slept in the same room, and if one of them had an idea in the night, he woke the other before he had time to forget. They then worked at it together. In the end, they had a machine that spun a smooth, strong, even thread. It was just what Need and Strutt wanted for stockings, and it was perfect for the warp threads in cloth as well.

The only problem left was that the machine needed a lot of power. They had to leave Nottingham, and build mills in the Pennines, where there were fast-flowing streams to drive water wheels. Because of this, Arkwright's invention was called the 'water frame'.

Soon, Arkwright left his partners and built his own mill at Cromford, the village we visited earlier. He built other mills as well. When he died, he had two and a half million pounds, and that would be worth thirty times as much today. The king knighted him, and he was made High Sheriff of Derbyshire. The humble barber had come a long way. He rode in his carriage, of course: in fact, he had several. However, he never forgot that his wife had burnt his first machine, and he punished her by keeping his promise! Every week, without fail, he gave her five shillings housekeeping money.

a water frame

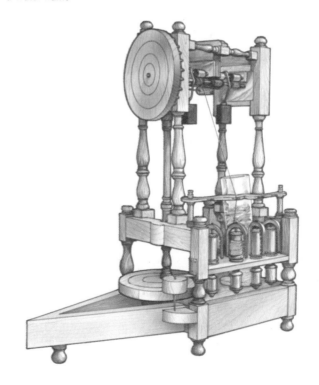

27

3 A Cotton Manufacturer in the Eighteenth Century

Francis Hookham is a cotton manufacturer. He lives in a splendid house in Manchester, and obviously he is a rich man. He has problems, though.

'My first worry is bringing my cotton from Liverpool. The Liverpool merchants unload it from the ships, and then it has to go into barges. In the estuary of the Mersey they often have trouble with the tides and headwinds. At Runcorn the boats join the Duke of Bridgewater's canal. The canal sometimes freezes in winter, and sometimes runs dry in summer. All the year round it is trying to carry more traffic than it should.

'Once the cotton is here, my men put it in my warehouse until we need it. I send some of it to my mill in the Pennines where they spin it into warp threads with water frames. That is the only part of the business which goes well. Most of my workers are scattered over southern Lancashire, and parts of Cheshire and Derbyshire. I have a depôt in many a village – a room in a pub, or something like that. We carry the cotton there on pack animals. Every Saturday, the spinners come and collect what they need from my agent. The next week, they bring back the thread they have spun and collect more cotton. My agent pays them for their work, of course.

'There are some lively arguments, I can tell you. The agent weighs the raw cotton, and the spinner must return the same weight of thread. Some of my agents are not very careful, though, and the spinners steal my cotton. There are good workers, who make fine, strong thread, but others make it too soft, too coarse, or, what's worse, quite uneven, and full of bumps and burs. Weavers can't use it, but if my agent refuses to pay, there is dreadful trouble. You can't rely on spinners to finish their work, either. Most of them are housewives, with a lot to do in their homes. At harvest time, the farmers need them, and they do no spinning for weeks. That is bad, when I have customers waiting for my goods. Lots of spinners are just lazy. They gossip all Monday and Tuesday, spin very little on Wednesday, and then try and do a week's work on Thursday and Friday. I pity their poor children on those days.' *'What about the weavers?'* 'They are even worse than the spinners. They come to the depôt on Saturday, as well, and my agent weighs out some yarn. It piles up in my warehouse, and I just cannot find weavers to take it all. I have tried paying them higher wages, but that's no good. If I give them more for each piece of cloth, they just do less work. Most of them have a bit of land, and a cow or a pig. They will cheerfully leave their looms to attend to them. They spend a lot of time drinking, as well. I think they are even more dishonest than the spinners, and steal a lot of my yarn. A good agent can always catch a thief, but not many of my agents are sharp enough. Another of their tricks is to make a good job of the few feet at the end of their roll of cloth, but take no care of the rest. What looks good work is often nothing of the kind.

'Well, in the end the finished cloth comes back to my warehouse. It is a dirty grey colour and we have to bleach it. That's a game, I can tell you. We soak it in water mixed with wood ash, we soak it in sour milk, and we peg it out in the bleach fields for the sun to do its work – that's when we have any sun. Usually, it takes six weeks. When it is pure white, we put it on pack animals and it goes all the way to London. The people down there print it. They know what colours and what patterns are in fashion, you see.' *'How far does a bit of cotton travel after it reaches Liverpool?'* 'That's hard to say, but some of it, two hundred miles, before it leaves my hands.' *'Why don't you bring all your workpeople into a factory?'* 'They would never come. No, they must have their freedom to stop work when they like, for a drink or a gossip. They have no sense of discipline.' *'But you have a mill in the Pennines.'* 'And do you know how I find the workers? I pay a few adults more than I can afford to persuade them to live in the wilds. For the rest, I have to go to the workhouses in the big cities like London and Birmingham. They give me orphan children as apprentices, and I send them out to the mill. As soon as they are twenty-one they can leave, and leave they do. It is really impossible to make people work regular hours in a factory.'

ell in his factory

A Cotton Factory in 1835

We will now go forward in time to 1835, and visit a cotton mill near Stockport, belonging to Mr. Orrell. He is very proud of his mill and is pleased to show us round.

The building is three hundred feet long, and fifty feet wide. It towers above us, for it is seven storeys high. We go into the ground floor. The noise is overpowering. 'These are my power looms,' shouts Mr. Orrell. 'I have a thousand of them. We have to put them on the ground floor, or they would shake the building to pieces.' The machines are in straight lines, and each one is working perfectly. Above them are shafts with pulleys. From the pulleys, big leather belts run down to the looms and drive them.

We go to a corner of a room where there is a staircase and a lift. We take the stairs, because the lift is for materials. The machines on the next floor are quieter. They make a singing noise which is quite pleasant. 'These are my throstles,' says Mr. Orrell. 'We call them that, because they sound like song thrushes. My father used water frames. These spin warp just as the water frames did, and work on the same lines. They are much better, though. For one thing, they are made of iron, not wood.' The second floor is the same as the first floor.

The third floor is for preparation. 'We bring the bales of cotton here and open them. The cotton is packed very tightly, so we have to loosen it with scutching machines. We also have to take out things like stones. The slaves in America who pack the cotton aren't too careful.' *'I thought the cotton came from Egypt and Turkey.'* 'A bit still does, but we could never have enough from there. They tell me that all the cotton cloth made in Lancashire last year would wrap round the equator eleven times.'

SCENE ON A COTTON PLANTATION. GATHERING COTTON.

'Before spinning, we have to comb the cotton. A woman wouldn't curl her hair before she had combed it, would she? Next, we draw it. Here you can see the drawing frames at work.' These machines are making the cotton into a long, loose roll, like a thin sausage, miles long. 'Now it is ready for spinning. Some of it goes down to the throstles, which you saw just now. The rest goes upstairs, to be spun into weft.'

On the fourth and fifth floors, Mr. Orrell has spinning machines called mules. Each one has a carriage, and a man pulls it forward about six feet. As he does so, hundreds of spindles turn busily, each twisting a thread of cotton so fine that it looks like cobweb. When the carriage is right forward, the man lets go, and it runs back of its own accord. The twisting stops, because the machine is winding up the length that it has just spun. 'These fine spinners are my most skilled men,' explains Mr. Orrell. 'They earn an enormous amount – about thirty shillings a week. They are a proud lot, too. Nearly every pub has a room for them with "Mule Spinners Only" on the door.'

We now go right to the top of the building. 'Here we do our finishing. Nasty smell, isn't there? That's chloride of lime. It's grand stuff for bleaching. We can make new cloth perfectly white in less than a day. Last of all, we print the cloth, and it is ready for the customer.' *'You don't send it to London for printing?'* 'We know as much about fashion as the London people, and with my new machines I can print the cotton at a fraction of the price, and in a fraction of the time that it took before. I buy bales of raw cotton, dyestuffs, and a few things like that, and I sell the finished cloth. All the work is done in my factory. My grandfather had spinners and weavers scattered over three counties. I don't know how he managed.' *'Do you have any problems with transport?'* 'It used to be hard bringing the cotton from Liverpool by canal, but we have a railway now. I hear

they are building another to London. That will be a great help.'

'Do you have trouble persuading people to work in your factory?' 'Most of the workers are women and children, as you saw. They do as they are told. The men are all highly skilled. I can afford to pay them good wages. They don't like the factory discipline though, especially when we are on a sixteen-hour day. We often work late. It is lucky we have gas lighting.'

Mr. Orrell now takes us down to the basement. Here two mighty steam engines are pounding and hissing away. 'Each engine is eighty horse power. I have two, because that gives a more even drive.' (If Mr. Orrell had known about bicycles, he could have explained that having one engine would be like riding a bicycle with one leg.)

Outside again, Mr. Orrell points proudly to his chimney. 'It is over 300 feet high. When it was new, and before we lit the fires, I took some of my friends up in the builders' hoist. I had a table up there, with some cakes and wine, as an extra surprise for them.'

33

5 Samuel Crompton

Samuel Crompton

Some of the most useful machines Mr. Orrell had in his cotton factory were his mules. The mule had been invented in the 1770s by Samuel Crompton.

Crompton was born in 1755, in Lancashire. His father had a farm, but it was not big enough to give the family a living. Like many others, they made up their income by spinning and weaving. Young Samuel had to do his share, and when he was sixteen his father gave him a spinning jenny. Samuel did not like his machine. As we have seen, jenny thread was soft, and full of 'bumps and burs'. Samuel, though, had heard about Arkwright's water frame, which used rollers. 'How would it be,' he thought, 'if I used the best ideas in both the spinning jenny and the water frame? I will make a machine better than either of them.' He did not find it easy, because he was not a mechanic. However, he was lucky in another way. The family lived at Hall i' th' Wood, a rambling old house with a big attic, which was just the place for Samuel to make his experiments.

After five years the machine was finished. Because it was part jenny and part water frame, Samuel called it a 'mule'. He took a pound of cotton and he spun some No. 40 thread. That meant he made 40 hanks from his pound of cotton, each 840 yards long. In all, it was nearly five miles of yarn. That may sound a lot,

mule spinning

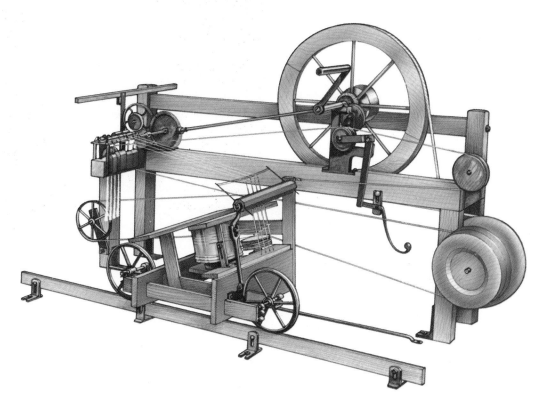

a mule

but any good spinner using a wheel or a jenny could do as well. What pleased Samuel, though, was that his yarn was smooth and strong, with no bumps and burs at all. The man who bought it was pleased, and a little puzzled. He was even more puzzled when Samuel came back later with some No. 60 yarn. In the end he was spinning No. 80 yarn, which is twice as fine as No. 40. Nothing like it had ever been seen before.

People now realised that Crompton must have a very special machine. Lots of visitors came to Hall i' th' Wood. Old Mrs. Crompton, she was by now a widow, tried to turn them away, but it was no use. Some even climbed the trees by the Hall, and looked through the attic windows with telescopes. Samuel wanted peace and quiet, so in the end he said that anyone could come and look at his machine on payment of one guinea. Several did so, and then went away and made mules of their own.

Later, other inventors improved the mule. Samuel's first machine spun forty threads at a time. Those in Orrell's factory each spun one thousand. Samuel worked his machine by hand, but the big machines needed steam power. By the 1840s most mules were 'self acting', which meant they worked all by themselves. A skilled mechanic had to stay with

them in case they went wrong, but the only other workers were a few children. Some of them were 'piecers' who joined any threads that broke: others were 'scavengers', who cleaned up the cotton dust. Samuel, as we have seen, was pleased to spin No. 80. The later mules spun No. 350. They made 165 miles of thread from each pound of cotton. No-one has ever invented a machine to spin better yarn than the mule. The only advantage modern machines have is that they are quicker.

What happened to Crompton? Between them, his visitors paid him about £50, and he used it to build a bigger mule for himself. He went on working in the attic at Hall i' th' Wood, but he did not earn a lot of money. In the meantime, men who had copied his machine were making fortunes. Some of Crompton's friends thought this was unfair, so they persuaded Parliament to give him £5,000. By now he was an old man, so he gave the money to his sons to start a business. They went bankrupt, and their father died in poverty.

What happened to all the women who had been working in their homes with spinning jennies? No-one wanted their yarn any more. The families had to manage as best they could without the wives' earnings.

6 Edmund Cartwright

After the invention of the water frame and the mule, there was so much yarn being spun, that it was hard to find enough weavers to make it into cloth. Employers had to pay weavers such high wages, that men like William Hobbs could afford expensive furniture for their homes. To show off, some went round with £5 notes stuck in their hat bands. Remember £5 of their money would be worth £150 today.

Then, in 1784, a clergyman called the Rev. Edmund Cartwright went on holiday to the fashionable little town of Matlock, in Derbyshire. At one of the parties, he met some cotton manufacturers from Manchester. They talked about the problems they had with their weavers. Cartwright knew nothing about making cotton cloth, but he said, 'You have spinning machines. Why doesn't someone invent a weaving machine?' They all laughed. 'Spinning is not too complicated,' one explained. 'Weaving is far more difficult. No-one could make a machine to do that.'

Cartwright had never seen a loom in his life, and he was no mechanic. Still, like many clergymen in those days, he had plenty of spare time. He decided to make a power loom, that is, a loom driven by a steam engine. A year later, he had finished his first machine. Sure enough, it worked, but it was clumsy, while the cloth it made was so coarse that it was only fit to make things like sacks. Cartwright now had a look at some ordinary looms, and was amazed to see how much better they were than his own. He studied them carefully, and copied many of their parts. Three years later, he had made a much better power loom, one that would weave good cloth. However, the machine had to be stopped so often that it was no faster than a handloom. If you had to adjust the chain of your

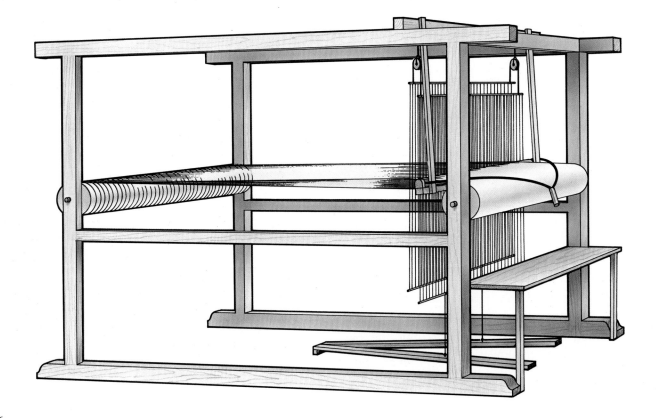

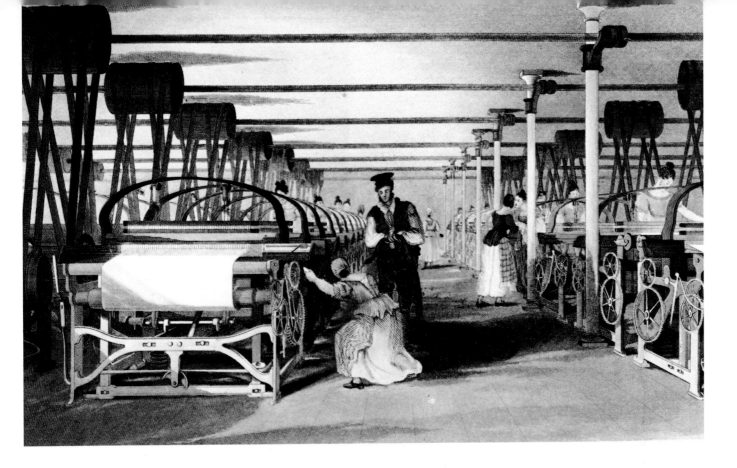

bicycle every hundred yards, you would find it quicker to walk. It was a bit like that.

In the end, Cartwright lost £30,000 on his loom, an enormous sum for those days. He then gave it up, but went on to make other inventions. None of them were much good. In the end, he did best as a farmer: he was never a good clergyman.

It was a long time before anyone else tried to make a power loom. However, in the 1820s a man called Horrocks succeeded. A boy or girl of fifteen could look after two of his looms and make four times as much cloth as a handloom weaver. It was Horrocks's machines that Mr. Orrell had in his factory.

We will now see what three different people thought of the power loom, and, indeed, all the new machines in the factories.

First, let us listen to a handloom weaver. 'When I was young, I could earn twenty-five or thirty shillings a week. Life was easy, too. I worked steadily enough from Tuesday to Friday, but I rarely did anything on Monday. Saturday was an easy day. I just went to the depôt to deliver my cloth, and collect more yarn. Now I can only earn seven shillings, and have to work fourteen hours a day, six days a week, even for that. My wages barely buy us enough bread. We can never afford new clothes. In the old days, my wife and I used to go out to the tea gardens or the theatre every Saturday. We always went to church on Sundays. Now, we cannot afford any amusements, and our clothes are so ragged that we are ashamed to go to church.'

An employer has something different to say. 'The handloom weavers are lazy and dishonest. When we employed them, they never did more than two or three good days' work in the week. I could not rely on them to finish their jobs to time. Many of them used to steal my yarn. Now, my machines work regular hours. I can tell my customers exactly when they will have their goods. No-one can steal from me, because all the work is done in my factory. We make twenty times as much as before. We have to sell the cloth a lot cheaper, but I still make handsome profits for myself. I can pay my skilled men good wages, too.'

Lastly, let us hear from a poor housewife. 'Now there are factories, cottons are wonderfully cheap. I can buy cloth in all sorts of pretty colours and patterns for less than a shilling a yard. I make my own dresses and I look as smart as any grand lady did thirty years ago. I can buy plain calico at threepence a yard for the children. That means I can afford to give them a change of clothing, so it is easy enough to keep them clean. My grandmother used to put her children to bed while she did the washing, and there they stayed until their clothes were dried.'

7 James Watt

James Watt's first experiment

None of Mr. Orrell's machines would have been any use without his two great steam engines. We must learn something about them.

The first man to build a steam engine that worked at all well was Thomas Newcomen, in 1709. It pumped water out of coal mines. At the top was a huge beam that rocked, like a seesaw. One end worked the pump, and at the other end was a piston in a cylinder. First, the weight of the pump rods pulled up the piston. At the same time, the boiler filled the cylinder with steam. Next, a valve cut off the steam and a jet of cold water shot into the cylinder. This condensed the steam, that is, cooled it, and turned it back into water. There was now a vacuum in the cylinder, so the weight of the atmosphere drove down the piston. This, in turn, pulled up the pump and sucked water out of the mine.

Newcomen's engines were useful, but they had a serious drawback. They burnt such a lot of fuel that only owners of coal mines could afford to run them. A man who had, for example, a copper mine, a cotton factory or an iron works badly needed a more econ-omical engine. The man who invented it was James Watt.

Watt was born at Greenock, in Scotland, in 1736. He trained to be an instrument mechanic, and took a job at Glasgow University. He had to look after all their scientific instruments. One day, a model Newcomen engine went wrong, and Watt repaired it. He was puzzled because it burnt a great deal of fuel, but did very little work. Watt was friendly with one of the University professors, Dr. Black. Black explained that the engine used such a lot of fuel because it had to heat the cylinder at every stroke. Much fuel would be saved if the cylinder stayed hot. But how was it possible to cool steam inside a hot cylinder? It would be like making ice-cream in the oven. Watt puzzled

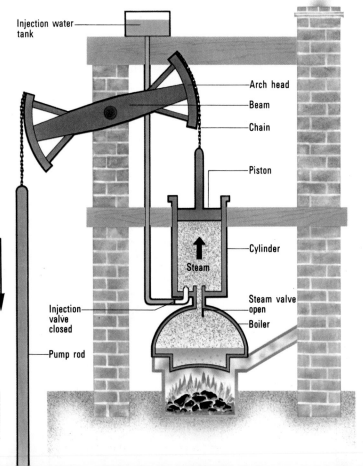

Injection water tank
Arch head
Beam
Chain
Piston
Cylinder
Steam
Injection valve closed
Steam valve open
Boiler
Pump rod

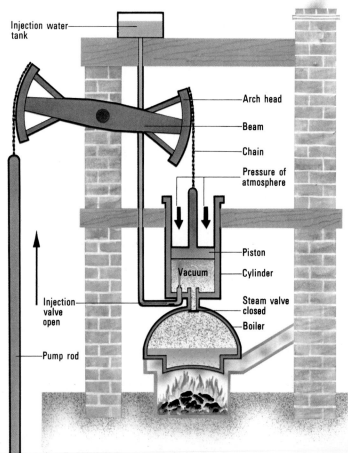

Injection water tank
Arch head
Beam
Chain
Pressure of atmosphere
Piston
Vacuum
Cylinder
Injection valve open
Steam valve closed
Boiler
Pump rod

and puzzled and then, one day, when he was out for a walk, the answer suddenly came to him. He made a separate chamber which he called a condenser. When the moment came to condense the steam, a valve opened, and the steam rushed into the condenser. Here a jet of water cooled it, and made a vacuum, so that the weight of the atmosphere drove down the piston just as before. The piston remained hot, instead of being cooled and heated at every stroke. The result was that the engine burnt a lot less fuel.

So far, Watt had only made a model. He wanted, of course, to build a full-sized engine, but he did not have the money. Luckily for him, he met a rich man from Birmingham called Matthew Boulton. Boulton owned the Soho works, a factory that produced metal goods. He employed many skilled craftsmen who were able to make the complicated parts that Watt needed. Soon Boulton and Watt were producing pumping engines. Men who had tin and copper mines in Cornwall were especially pleased, because they had to bring all their coal from South Wales, and it was expensive.

Watt now wanted to make an engine that would drive machinery. He worked hard at his plans, and in the end he succeeded. These Boulton and Watt engines were a great help to people with factories. Mr. Orrell explains: 'Any mill needs 100 horse power to drive its machinery. We have water wheels as powerful as that, but there are not many places you can put them. You need large, fast-flowing streams to drive them. Before the steam engine, people like Arkwright and Strutt built their mills up in the Pennine valleys. You can imagine how hard that made transport. Besides, it was almost impossible to persuade workers to live in those out of the way places. Thanks to the steam engine, I was able to build my mill down here in Stockport. Lots of my friends have mills in and around Manchester. There is no problem finding workers in the big towns. Also, transport is easy, especially since the railways came. We are very grateful to James Watt.'

Watt was, indeed, a great inventor. Unfortunately, he was a mean, miserable man. But for Boulton, other men would have stolen his ideas, and he would have died a poor man, like so many inventors. As it was, he made a fortune, but he would never help the firm with his own money. It was always Boulton who found the cash. Watt was too selfish even to give his own son a large enough allowance. The young man knew better than ask his father for money. He went to Boulton, who gave him all he needed.

The picture on page 38 is of a Newcomen pump; the picture below shows James Watt's improved model.

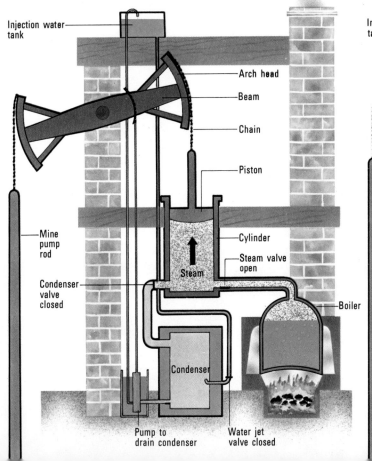

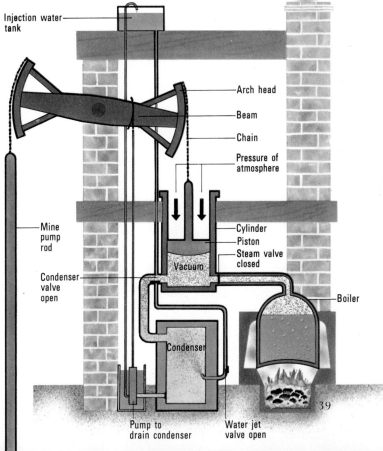

The Village becomes a Town

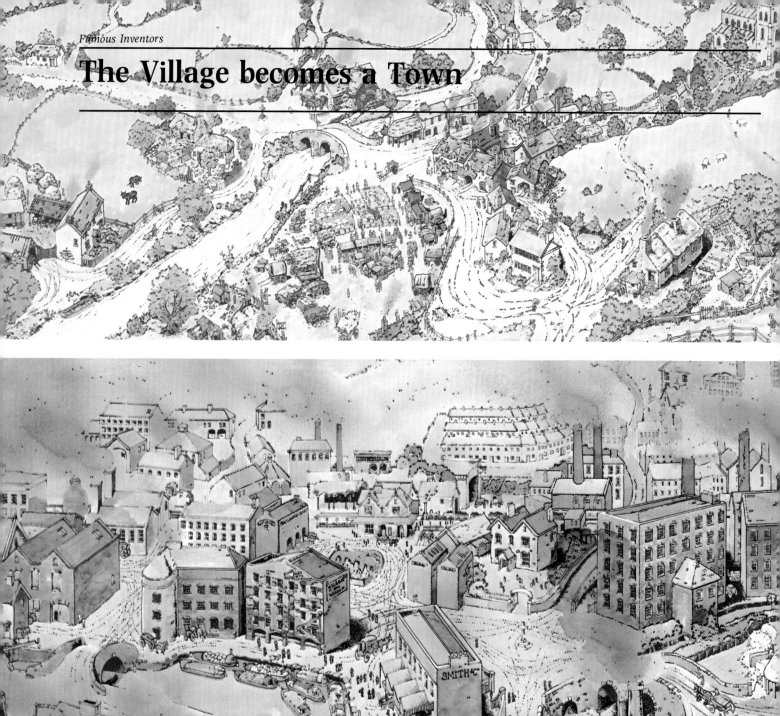

Work Section

Understand Your Work

1 The Cotton Village
1 Why was there no factory in an eighteenth-century cotton village?
2 What are warp and weft?
3 Who invented the flying shuttle? When? What advantage did it have?
4 Why did weavers dislike the flying shuttle, at first? What happened to the inventor?
5 What problem did the flying shuttle create?
6 How long does William Hobbs spend weaving? What does he do the rest of the day?
7 How many threads did a spinning jenny spin?
8 Who invented the spinning jenny? When?
9 Why was the spinning jenny unpopular, at first?
10 What happened to the inventor?

2 Richard Arkwright
1 How do warp threads need to be made? Why?
2 Where is Cromford? What buildings were there in the village?
3 What was Arkwright's first job? What did he decide to do, in order to become rich?
4 What idea did Arkwright copy from Lewis Paul?
5 Why did Arkwright go to Nottingham?
6 Whom did Arkwright meet in Nottingham? Why did they welcome him?
7 Give two uses for the thread spun by Arkwright's machine.
8 Where did Arkwright and his partners build their mills? Why?
9 What name was given to Arkwright's machine? Why?
10 What happened to Arkwright in later life?

3 The Cotton Manufacturer
1 Why was it difficult to transport cotton from Liverpool to Manchester?
2 Why does Mr. Hookham send some of his cotton to the Pennines?
3 Where are the rest of his workers?
4 Explain how the cotton is given out to the spinners and the thread collected.
5 What problems are there with the spinners?
6 How is thread given out to the weavers and the cloth collected?
7 What problem did the spinning jenny and the water frame create?
8 What happened to cotton cloth after it had been woven?
9 How would it have helped Mr. Hookham if all his people had worked in a factory? Why does he say this is impossible?
10 How does Mr. Hookham find workers for his mill in the Pennines?

4 A Cotton Factory in 1835
1 What is on the ground floor of Mr. Orrell's factory? Why are they there?
2 What machines are on the first floor? What work do they do? What machines did they replace?
3 On what floor are the scutching machines and drawing frames? What work do they do?
4 What machines are there on the fourth and fifth floors? What work do they do?
5 How is bleaching done? How long does it take? How long had it taken in the old days? (See p. 28.)
6 What work, once done in London, is now done in the factory?
7 Why does Mr. Orrell feel his work is better organised than his grandfather's?
8 How has transport improved?
9 Why has Mr. Orrell been able to find workers?
10 What drives Mr. Orrell's machines?

5 Samuel Crompton and the Mule
1 How did Crompton's father make a living?
2 Why did Crompton want to make a spinning machine?
3 Where did Crompton work?
4 Which two machines did he copy? Why was his machine called a mule?
5 What kind of thread did the mule spin?
6 Why did Crompton have many unwanted visitors? How did he get rid of them?
7 Name four ways in which the mule was improved.
8 What workers looked after mules?
9 Why did Parliament give Crompton £5,000? What happened to him in the end?
10 What happened to the women who used spinning jennies? (Have a look at p. 18 as well as p. 35.)

6 The Reverend Edmund Cartwright and the Power Loom
1 Why had it become necessary to invent a power loom?
2 Why did it seem impossible to do so?
3 What was wrong with Cartwright's first machine? What was wrong with his second machine?
4 What happened to Cartwright in the end?
5 Who, finally, perfected the power loom?
6 What advantages did the power loom have over the hand loom?
7 What happened to the handloom weavers as a result of the invention of the power loom?
8 How did power looms help employers?
9 Why could employers still make good profits, even though cloth was a lot cheaper?
10 How did the cotton factories help ordinary housewives and their children?

7 The Steam Engine
1 When did Newcomen build his steam engine? What work did it do?
2 Who were the only people that could afford Newcomen engines? Why?

3 Who also wanted steam engines?
4 When and where was James Watt born?
5 Who helped him with the invention of his steam engine?
6 Where did Matthew Boulton live? What did he own?
7 How did Boulton help Watt? (See p. 39.)
8 What work did the first Boulton and Watt engines do? Who bought them?
9 How did Watt improve his engine? Why were the improved engines valuable for cotton manufacturers?
10 What kind of a man was Watt?

Use Your Imagination

1 William Hobbs had a son called George who took over from his father. Write the story of his life. (1, 6)
2 You visited a cotton village in 1780, and have come back in 1830. What changes do you notice? (1, 5, 6)
3 You are Richard Arkwright as a young man. Say what plans you are making for the future. (2)
4 You are Mrs. Arkwright in her old age. Write the story of your life. (2)
5 Write a list of rules Mr. Hookham might have drawn up for his workers. (3)
6 It is 1780. Follow some cotton from the day it arrives in Britain until it is part of a finished piece of cloth. Say what happens to it at each stage. Illustrate your answer with a sketch map showing Liverpool, Manchester, the Pennines and London. (1, 3)
7 Follow a piece of cotton through Mr. Orrell's factory. Say what is happening to it at each stage. Be sure you start on the correct floor of the factory. (4)
8 What changes do you think Mr. Orrell's factory made in Stockport? (4)
9 Write a report for a newspaper describing events at Hall i' th' Wood immediately after Crompton had invented the mule. (5)
10 You are Samuel Crompton in his old age. Write the story of your life. What regrets have you? (5)
11 Write an advertisement for one of Horrocks's power looms. (6)
12 You are Matthew Boulton. Explain to a factory owner why he will do better to use one of your steam engines, rather than a water wheel. (7)
13 A cotton manufacturer of the 1830s and his grandfather discuss the changes that have taken place in the industry. Write what they say. (All)
14 Make a list of the inventors in the chapter. Which ones made a lot of money out of their inventions, and which did not? Try to decide why this was. (All)
15 How different would our lives be today if cloth was still made on spinning wheels and handlooms? (All)

Further Work

1 Find out more about the ways spinning and weaving were done. If your school has a loom, ask to see how it works.
2 Read about the Midlands stocking industry.
3 Many goods were made in people's homes, apart from cotton cloth. Find out if this happened in your area.
4 What changes have been made in the textile industries since the 1830s?
5 Find out more about child workers in factories. Start by reading Section Six of Chapter Four.
6 Read more about Edmund Cartwright.
7 Find pictures of eighteenth- and early nineteenth-century clothing.
8 Read more about Thomas Newcomen.
9 Which inventors improved the steam engine, after James Watt?
10 Choose another industry which may interest you, e.g. engineering. Find out what inventions were made there.

Chapter Three   Transport

1 Transport in the Early Eighteenth Century

Until about two hundred years ago, most roads were like farm tracks. That was all they needed to be, since few people travelled long distances. Farmers drove their carts to and from their fields, and were happy to lumber along at two miles an hour. They did not worry if the roads were rough.

It was the duty of the people in each village to take care of their own roads. In 1555 Parliament made a law to say what they should do. The local farmers had to choose one of their number to be Surveyor of Highways. He could call on his poor neighbours to work on the roads for six days a year, without wages; he could make richer people lend their horses, carts and tools, free of charge.

The system did not work well. We can see why if we watch a gang road-mending. The Surveyor has sent for five men, and they have come most unwillingly. They lounge about and do as little as they can. A farmer was supposed to send some picks, some shovels and a horse and cart, but they arrived very late. There are not enough tools, while some of them are broken. The cart is worn out: the horse is old and tired. The Surveyor is not a trained Surveyor at all, but an ordinary farmer. He is angry because he has had to leave his own work, and he knows nothing about road building. His main problem is to drain away the water that makes the ground soft under the road. In some parts he has made the road very high in the middle, like the roof of a house. This lets the rain run off, but carts must keep to the centre of the road, otherwise they are in danger of tipping sideways. Even so, there is one patch that is always giving way, however much stone they put on it. Here the Surveyor decides to make the road as one switch-back after another, with a drain running across it at the bottom of each dip. It is lucky no-one wants to drive a cart at more than two miles an hour.

There were a few people who needed to travel long distances. You can imagine what it was like to go, perhaps, a hundred miles along cart tracks, and not

very good ones at that. There were stage coaches, but they ran only in summer. They had to be built very strongly, without springs, which meant they were most uncomfortable. It took a coach about ten days to go from London to Edinburgh. The only way to travel at all quickly was on horseback.

Some people had goods to carry. Woollen manufacturers, for example, needed to send sacks of wool and bales of cloth all over the country. They might use stage waggons, but they went at only half the pace of the coaches, and they, too, could only travel in summer. As with people, it was best for goods to go on horses. However, a pack-horse can only carry just over a hundredweight. If he has a cart on a good road, a horse can pull two tons.

The only way to move heavy goods long distances was by river. Even here there were problems. A Severn boatman will tell you about his work. 'My vessel is called a "trow". She is built like a proper ship, and is about sixty feet long and twenty wide. She has one big, square sail, though we can only use that when the wind is right behind us. We go up the Severn as far as Shrewsbury, but often we have to stay there for

days, or even weeks. The river runs dry and is too shallow. Sooner or later, though, down comes the rain, and we have a "fresh" which is a good rush of water. It will carry us merrily all down to Gloucester. Below Gloucester life is a bit easier, because there is a high tide every fortnight. We get by as best we can, with the current, the wind and the tides. They can't be against us all the time. They are often enough, though, and then my mates and I have to walk along the bank, pulling the boat. That's hard, slow work, I can tell you.'

One great problem was how to carry coal to London. Many people lived in the capital and there were not enough forests near at hand, to supply wood for fuel. Luckily, the Durham coalfield is close to the sea. Hundreds of little ships called brigs used to sail to the River Tyne for cargoes of coal. They carried it to London and, indeed, to places all along the coast as far as Lyme Regis, in Dorset. They were tough ships, with tough crews. The government was glad they were there because, in time of war, they pressganged the sailors into the Royal Navy.

2 Turnpike Roads

John Macadam   Thomas Telford

In the 1660s the people of Stanton in Hertfordshire were in despair. Every day large waggons came through their village, loaded with grain for London. As we saw in the last chapter, village folk did not expect many strangers to use their roads. At Stanton, though, strangers used them a great deal and damaged them badly. The roads became so bad that the magistrates fined the inhabitants and ordered them to work twelve days a year on their roads, instead of six. The people thought that the men who ruined the roads should pay for them, so they complained to Parliament. Parliament agreed with them. It allowed them to put up a toll gate and collect money from passing traffic to pay for repairs.

After 1700 there was more and more traffic everywhere, so many places had the same problem as Stanton. When that happened, important local people, like farmers and landowners, joined together to form a 'Turnpike Trust'. Parliament then gave them permission to put up gates and collect tolls, just as it had done for Stanton. The money paid for new roads called 'turnpike roads'. They had the name 'turnpike' from the 'pikes' or 'spikes' they put on top of their gates to stop people on horseback from jumping over.

By 1830 there were about 1,000 Turnpike Trusts in Britain. Most of them had about ten or twelve miles of road, though some had many more. The Bristol Trust looked after 173 miles of road.

Turnpike Trusts expected a lot of traffic, so they employed Surveyors who knew how to build roads properly. One such man was Thomas Telford. Telford prepared the bed of a new road carefully, making sure that every inch was properly drained. Roads collapse if the soil under them is wet and soggy. Next, he laid a good foundation of large stones. On top of those he put a layer of gravel, to make a smooth surface. Telford's most famous road was the one he built for the Government, from London to Holyhead. Holyhead was important, because it was there that the passenger ships sailed to Dublin. Telford built bridges as well. His most famous is the handsome suspension bridge over the Menai Straits. He was so pleased when it was finished that he kept riding backwards and forwards over it.

Another important road builder was John Macadam. Like Telford he drained his road bed carefully, but he did not put down heavy, expensive foundations. First came a layer of medium-sized stones and then a layer of smaller ones. The traffic finished the work. It ground the stones together making a fine powder that filled the gaps, and then pounded the road down so that the surface was waterproof. Macadam showed that as long as the ground below the road was dry, there was no need for foundations. His roads did not last as long as Telford's, but they were a lot cheaper.

Macadam employed women and old men to break stones. Doing it his way was not hard work. You sat down, and used a little hammer, with a long handle. A woman could crack as many stones like that, as two strong men using sledge hammers. It was important to make the stones the right size. Macadam told his workers that a stone should just fit in the mouth, so one day he was angry to see an old man making his stones much too large. He soon found the reason. The old man had no teeth.

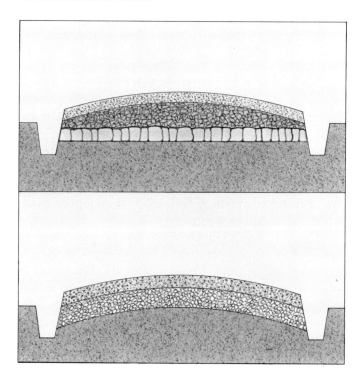

When coach owners saw the new roads, they made much better coaches. They were light, well sprung, and comfortable. They would rattle along at twenty miles an hour and keep an average speed of twelve miles an hour. People could now go to places in a fifth of the time it had taken before. London to Edinburgh, for example, now took two days, instead of ten.

Coaching inns became important. It was at an inn that you bought your ticket, waited for the coach, had a meal, or slept the night. It was also the place where coachmen collected and dropped mail. Each inn, then, did the work of a railway station, hotel and post office. The most valuable job, though, was to change the horses. The ostlers had the four fresh horses ready before the coach arrived and could change them, with all their harness and buckles, in less than two minutes.

Turnpike Roads

a scene at a tollgate

3 Canals

In 1760, Francis, Duke of Bridgewater was an un-happy man. He was deeply in love with a young lady, but she did not like him at all. He felt he had to do something to help him forget how miserable he was. It so happened that he owned some coal mines at the village of Worsley in Lancashire. He sold the coal in Manchester. Unfortunately, there was a lot of water in the mines, which made them dangerous. Also, it was difficult to take the coal to Manchester, even though it was only seven miles away. There was no river, and the roads were bad, so they had to use pack-horses.

Then the Duke had an idea. Why not build a canal from Worsley to Manchester, filling it with water from the mines? He would drain his mines and have good transport for his coal, at the same time. But how was the Duke to build the canal? People knew about improving rivers by dredging them, making locks and building towpaths, but hardly anyone knew about canals. However, the Duke heard of a man called James Brindley. Brindley was a clever millwright. He knew how to make such things as mill dams, sluice gates, and leats. Leats are the channels which take water to the wheel. Brindley had no education, so when he had a problem he did not sit down with a pen

the Duke of Bridgewater

and paper. Instead, he went to bed and lay staring at the ceiling until he had the answer. It was Brindley who helped the Duke build his canal.

You can see from the map, that the canal ran from Worsley to Barton. Here it met the valley of the River Irwell. This was difficult, so the Duke asked Brindley what to do. Brindley built him an aqueduct over the river. You can see it in the picture. Later, aqueducts became common enough, but the one at Barton was the first and people were amazed. They were fascinated to see one boat sailing over the head of another.

When the Bridgewater Canal was finished, the people of Manchester were able to buy coal at half the price they had paid before.

Now other people wanted canals. One was Josiah Wedgwood, who made expensive pottery at Etruria, in Staffordshire. He used china clay which came from Cornwall by sea to the Mersey, and flintstone, which came from near Hull. He badly wanted a canal to join the rivers Trent and Mersey so he, and some other men, asked Brindley to build one. Brindley agreed, and in 1777 the Grand Trunk Canal, as they called it, was opened. It was much more difficult to make than the Bridgewater Canal, for it was 100 miles long, it had 76 locks and five aqueducts. There was also a tunnel two miles long at Harecastle. It had no towpath, so the boatmen had to lie down on boards that stuck out from the barges and 'walk' with their feet against the sides of the tunnel.

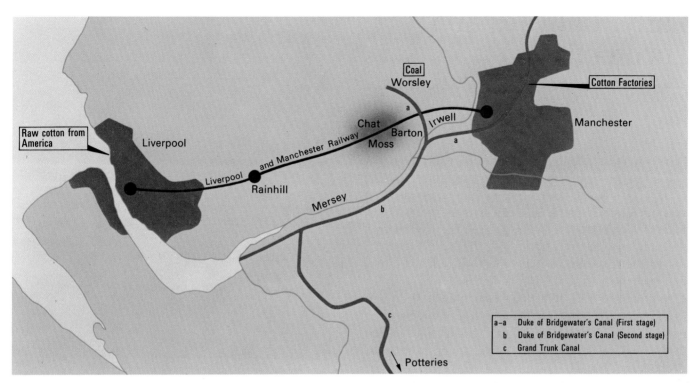

the Bridgewater canal and the canal system

Brindley died of work and worry, five years before the Grand Trunk was finished. Many other men were to die as well, from accidents. The work was so dangerous that two navvies were killed for every mile of canal made in this country.

Soon, other canals were built to join the Grand Trunk to the River Severn, and to the River Thames. You can see from the map how many places they joined. Then, in the 1790s, canals were built all over Great Britain, except where there were mountains. Nearly every big town had a canal to carry its heavy goods, especially coal.

There were problems with canals. Some of the boatmen were expert thieves. For example, they could open a sack of sugar, take out a few handfuls, replace them with earth, and then stitch up the sack, so that no-one knew it had been touched. The customer was the first to find out, for the small amount of earth, spoiled all the sugar. The weather made difficulties. In a long, hot summer, canals ran dry. In cold weather, they froze. Also, the boats were slow. The horses just plodded along at three miles an hour, so it was no use going by canal, if you were in a hurry. Passengers went by stage coach instead.

However, canals were ideal for heavy goods. One horse, pulling a canal barge, can move as much coal as 400 pack animals.

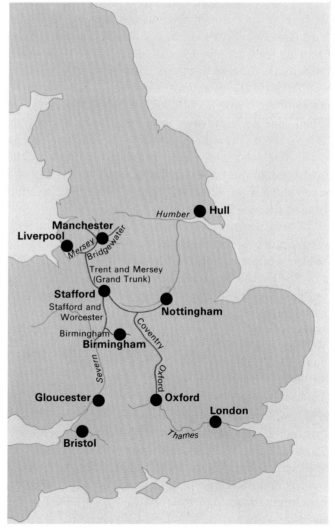

4 Early Railways and Locomotives

Have you ever tried to push a wheelbarrow? If so, you will know how difficult it is when the ground is soft, or when the wheel keeps hitting stones. However, if you put down a plank you can trundle your wheelbarrow along it quite easily. That is the idea behind the railway.

In the sixteenth century, men who owned mines and quarries laid wooden rails for their waggons. To keep the rails the right distance apart they nailed them to sleepers. To stop the sleepers from moving they packed stones between them, which they called 'ballast'. A modern railway is still made from rails, sleepers and ballast.

By the eighteenth century there were many waggon ways, some of them as much as twenty miles long. Their builders soon saw it was important to keep them as level as possible. In some places they made embankments, and in others, cuttings and tunnels.

To pull the waggons they used horses. On a waggon way, one horse could draw eight tonnes. On a bad road he could only manage a tonne and a half. Where there was a downhill slope, the waggon ran by itself. The man had a ride, keeping his hand on the brake, while the horse walked behind. At the top of a steep slope, they sometimes put a steam engine, that hauled the waggons up with a rope.

There were many waggon ways on the Durham coalfield. They carried the coal from the mines to the collier brigs, that you read about on page 45.

The trouble with wooden rails was that they wore out quickly, so in the late eighteenth century, they made them of iron. Some of the early iron rails were known as 'plates', because they were wide and flat We still call a man who puts down railway lines a 'platelayer'.

While some men were building waggon ways, others were making steam engines. The early steam engines were enormous and had to be bolted to the ground. They pumped water and drove machinery. Then, one day in 1784, the Vicar of Redruth in Cornwall was coming home in the dark when he heard a puffing and snorting. Next, he saw a dreadful monster, breathing smoke and fire, and he fled, quite sure the devil was after him. What he had seen was a steam

locomotive – that is, a steam engine that moves itself. It was the work of William Murdoch.

Another inventor was Richard Trevithick. His first steam locomotive went on the road, like Murdoch's, but he soon made one that ran on rails. It was for a coal mine in South Wales. He also amused the crowds in London with his 'Catch Me Who Can'. At first, the rails broke because they were not meant for anything as heavy as a locomotive. However, engineers made stronger rails, and the steam railway was born.

Perhaps the most famous railway inventor was George Stephenson. He built a number of locomotives for coal mines, and then came his big chance. In 1820 a woollen mill in the little town of Darlington burnt down. Many people lost their jobs, and a man called Edward Pease felt sorry for them. He thought that if he could build a railway to carry coal from the mines in South Durham it would help people start factories both in Darlington and in Stockton. The story goes that Stephenson tramped to Darlington to call on Pease. Pease nearly sent the stranger away, but he suddenly changed his mind and saw him. Pease was so impressed that he asked Stephenson to engineer the railway.

The Stockton to Darlington line opened in 1825. Above Darlington they used horses, stationary engines and gravity inclines, but between Darlington and Stockton they used locomotives.

the opening of the Stockton to Darlington line in 1825

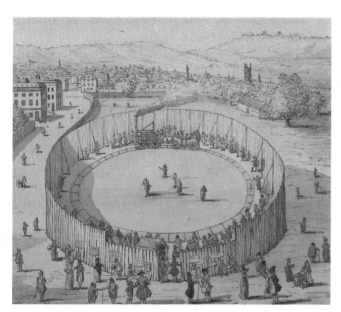

Trevithick's locomotive

Stephenson did not know how far apart to put the rails, so he measured the local waggon ways to see what gauge they were. He found that, on average, they were 4′ 8½″, so that was the measurement he used. It is a very odd one, but most other railways in Britain copied it, and so did railways all over the world.

Many folk did not like the new line. Stephenson had to change the route he had planned because the Duke of Cleveland said the trains would drive away his foxes. People who owned plantations of pine trees were angry because the locomotives sent out showers of sparks. When the engines had no trucks to pull, their drivers went at top speed, which was twelve miles an hour. This frightened any horses that were near, so the drivers were ordered to go at no more than five miles an hour. Most people, though, were glad to have the cheap coal the railway brought them.

5 The Liverpool and Manchester Railway

On September 15th, 1830, a train set out from Liverpool to Manchester. It carried a lot of important people, including the Duke of Wellington, and a cabinet minister, William Huskisson. It was the official opening of the railway and Huskisson was delighted. He had done a lot to encourage the building of the line. The train stopped in a cutting, and Huskisson could not resist getting out to chat to people in other carriages. He was talking to the Duke of Wellington when someone shouted, 'The Rocket is coming!' Sure enough that famous locomotive was hurtling along the other track. Huskisson jumped to the side of the cutting, but did not feel safe. He jumped back again and tried to climb into the Duke's carriage. He was too late. The 'Rocket' ran into him, breaking his leg, and he died a little later. No-one was able to enjoy themselves after a tragedy like that. None the less, September 15th, 1830, was still an important day, for it saw the opening of the first modern railway. Why had it been built?

The Liverpool and Manchester Railway

In the early part of the nineteenth century, Manchester became an important town for the manufacture of cotton cloth. The raw cotton came from America to Liverpool, and then went the thirty miles from Liverpool to Manchester by barge. In summer, the canals sometimes ran dry and in winter they sometimes froze. What was worse, their owners charged high tolls.

In 1822, the merchants of Liverpool thought they had had enough trouble from the waterways so they decided to build a railway to Manchester. They formed a company and chose George Stephenson to be their engineer.

Stephenson's first task was to plan the exact route for the line, which meant he had to make a survey. Surveyors have to work carefully, with complicated instruments, and it is important to leave them in peace. Unfortunately, there were many people who did not want the railway, including two noblemen. They all objected, just as we do today if there is to be a motor-

the Olive Mount cutting

way close to our homes. They said that fields anywhere near the line would become black and useless, that cows would no longer give milk, and that sheep would no longer have lambs. Ignorant people believed these stories. Farmers turned bulls and dogs on the railway men. The two noblemen paid thugs to attack them. Instead of proper surveyors, Stephenson had to employ professional boxers! In the end, though, they finished their work, and Parliament passed an Act giving the company permission to build its line.

Now there were other problems. The people of Liverpool refused to have a noisy railway, so Stephenson had to build a tunnel, over a mile long, under the town. The workmen met a lot of water which threatened to drown them. There was also soft sand which fell on them, nearly burying them alive. However, engineers had learnt a lot about making tunnels from the canal builders, so they finished it eventually.

Near Manchester there was a marsh called Chat Moss. It was impossible to dig through it, and if you tipped in stone it just vanished away. Stephenson told his men to lay hurdles on the moss and pile stones on them. Then came more hurdles, and more stones, so that it was like making sandwiches, one on top of the other. The hurdles stopped the stones escaping, and although many layers sank into the marsh, in the end there was a good, firm bed for the railway.

a train crosses Chat Moss

The Directors of the Company had still not decided what was to pull their trains. Many of them thought they should have a number of stationary engines, drawing the trucks with ropes. Stephenson said they should have locomotives. How could they be sure, though, that the locomotives would be good enough for the work? The Company decided to hold a competition with a prize of £500, which would be about £15,000 in modern money. The trials were held at Rainhill in 1829, and many people came to watch. Their favourite locomotive was the 'Novelty', built by two London men, Braithwaite and Ericsson. It shot up and down the line at 30 miles an hour. This was the first time anyone had seen a machine go as fast as a horse could gallop, so the crowd was amazed. Unfortunately, the 'Novelty' kept breaking down. Then George Stephenson and his son Robert brought out their locomotive, the 'Rocket'. It, too, ran at 30 miles an hour and what is more, it did not break down. The Directors gave the prize to the Stephensons.

As we have seen, the Liverpool and Manchester line was finished in 1830. It was such a success that people began to build railways in many other places. By 1850 all our important cities were joined together, and Britain had the first public railway system in the world.

the *Novelty* and the *Rocket*

6 Sailing Ships

Quite likely you have visited the clipper ship *Cutty Sark* at Greenwich. If so, you will have seen her tall masts with their complicated rigging and long spars. They give you some idea of the great spread of canvas she carried. In all it was 32,000 square feet, and that was not a great deal for a clipper. The larger clippers had 50,000 square feet, which is bigger than a football pitch. You will also have seen the *Cutty Sark*'s finely pointed bows, and graceful stern. Clearly, she was built for speed. Indeed, 'clipper' comes from a Dutch word 'klepper', which means a fast horse.

Sailing ships had not always been like that. In the eighteenth century they were rather like floating shoe boxes. Owners cared more about the amount of cargo their ships could carry, than how fast they could sail. The best of these old ships belonged to the East India Company. They were as well armed as men-of-war.

An East Indiaman once captured a French frigate, and another time a group of them fought with some French battleships. On the other hand, they often took six months to go to India, and up to a year to reach China.

There were few changes in the early nineteenth century until 1841, when an American called John Griffith designed a ship with fine lines and tall, sloping masts to carry a huge spread of sail. They were the plans of the first clipper. The New York shipowners were not interested. The hull was not roomy enough, and all the sails would have needed a large crew to work them. Within a few years, though, shipowners were begging Griffith to build them clippers. What had happened to make them change their minds?

For centuries, China had been unwilling to trade with other countries, but in 1842 she lost a war against Britain. Britain made her open her ports to

foreigners. The most important thing China had to sell was tea, and the ship that brought in the first of the new crop had the best price for its cargo. Griffith's ships were ideal for the tea trade. Then, about 1850, prospectors found gold in both California and in Australia. Men wanted to go to these places as quickly as possible, so they went on American clippers, because they were much faster than any British ships.

Not surprisingly, the British wanted clippers of their own. In 1852 an Englishman, Richard Green, built the *Challenger*. On her first voyage from China she raced the American ship *Challenge*, and beat her by two days. Soon there were many British clippers, most of them better than the Americans. The American builders used their native softwoods, which were cheap, but they became waterlogged, and the ships wore out in ten years. The planks moved so much the sailors joked that if you sat on the deck they would pinch your bottom. The British used teak or mahogany planks on iron ribs, so their ships lasted much longer. The *Cutty Sark* had a working life of 52 years.

A clipper ship in full sail was a wonderful sight, but the crew had a hard time. Sailing ships followed the winds, so they were often hundreds of miles out in the middle of the ocean. They could go for many days without sight of land, or even another ship. Often, storms battered them, especially off Cape Horn. To most of us it would be an adventure to climb the rigging of the *Cutty Sark* as she lies in dry dock. The sailors had to go aloft during gales and snowstorms while the top of the mast swayed as much as two hundred feet from side to side. They then had to work their way along the spars on footropes, to haul in enormous sails that might be sodden with water, or stiff with frost. At other times their ship could lie becalmed for days together in the heat of the tropics. For food, the men had little more than salt fish and ship's biscuits, though after 1850 they also had a ration of lime-juice each day, which stopped them developing scurvy. The sailor slept on a narrow bunk in the crowded forecastle. His mattress was stuffed with straw, so he called it a 'donkey's breakfast'. In spite of the hardship and danger he earned only £4 a month.

unloading tea

Sailing Ships

As more and more clippers were built, there was keen competition to bring the first cargo of tea to London. The winning ship had a valuable prize. In 1866 there was an especially exciting race when five ships left the Chinese port of Foochow within thirty hours of each other. The voyage was 14,000 miles, and took 99 days, but at the end the two leading ships, the *Taeping* and the *Ariel*, were racing neck and neck up the English Channel. *Ariel* reached Deal first. This was where clippers had to take in their sails, so that steam tugs could tow them up the Thames.

Taeping arrived just afterwards and was lucky to have the more powerful tug. She docked first by just twenty minutes. Her captain and crew were sportsmen, though, and shared their prize money with the men from the *Ariel*.

7 Steam Ships

Isambard Kingdom Brunel

One day in 1835, the Directors of the Great Western Railway Company met to talk about the new railway they were planning. It was to run from London to Bristol, which was over a hundred miles. This was in the early days of railways, and some of the Directors thought the line would be far too long. At this, the Company's engineer said, 'Why not make it longer? We could build a steamship to sail from Bristol to New York, and call her the Great Western.' The engineer's name was Isambard Kingdom Brunel.

Brunel's father, Marc, had fled to England during the French Revolution. Here, he became a famous engineer. Isambard was born in 1806, and he, too, became an engineer. When he was only twenty-three he designed the handsome suspension bridge at Clifton, near Bristol. In 1833 the Great Western Railway Company chose him as their engineer. This gave him an enormous amount of work, but he could not forget his dream. He was determined that one day, people should travel all the way from London to New York by steam.

There had been small steamships for a long time. By 1830 there were 300 of them in Britain. They took passengers around the coast and over to France and Ireland. Sailing ships with engines in them had already

the *Great Western*

crossed the Atlantic, but they had only used their engines part of the way. The problem in those days was that steam engines burnt a lot of fuel. A ship crossing the Atlantic would need more coal than she could carry. Brunel saw that the answer to the problem was to have bigger ships. A ship that is four times as large as another will use only twice as much fuel. It is a bit like buses and cars. A bus carries twenty times as many passengers as a car, but uses only five times as much fuel. Consequently, Brunel's *Great Western* was 1,340 tonnes, about twice the size of any other steamship.

The *Great Western* was launched at Bristol in 1837, and was then towed to the Thames to have her engines and all her other equipment fitted. Meanwhile, a rival company in Liverpool was also building a large steamer. They soon realized that the *Great Western* would be finished first, so they chartered a ship called the *Sirius*. She was only half the size of the *Great Western* but her owners thought that if she had some alterations, she might just cross the Atlantic. She, too, went to the Thames for changes to be made.

the *Sirius*

On March 28th, 1838, the *Sirius* was ready. She steamed past the *Great Western*, which was still not quite finished. Brunel did not lose heart, though. He knew the *Sirius* would have to lose a lot of time at Cork in Ireland, taking on coal. And he knew his own ship was much faster. Everyone worked hard, and on March 31st the *Great Western* set sail. Brunel was sure she would catch the *Sirius*. Within two hours, though, she was on fire. As Brunel rushed to the boiler room to see what was happening, he fell 28 feet and lay unconscious, his head in a pool of water. He would have been killed, but he landed on another man, who broke his fall, and pulled him out of the water. As it was, he was so badly injured that he had to go ashore.

The fire was put out, but it was twelve hours before the *Great Western* was sailing again. She went to Bristol where she took on coal, supplies and seven passengers. Fifty people had cancelled their bookings when they heard about the fire. At last, on April 8th, the *Great Western* set out for America. The *Sirius* had already left Cork on April 4th.

April 22nd, 1838, was an exciting day for the people of New York. In the morning, they heard that the first steamer had crossed the Atlantic from England, and they went to cheer her. She was a handsome vessel, with a figure-head of a dog holding a star — the *Sirius*. Then, in the afternoon another steamer twice the size of the first arrived, and was also cheered. For all her late start, the *Great Western* was only a few hours behind her rival.

Though he had lost the race, Brunel had proved that big steamers were better than small ones. It was not just that they were faster. The *Sirius* had burnt all her coal, while the *Great Western* still had enough for another 1,000 miles. She crossed the Atlantic regularly, while the *Sirius* was soon back where she belonged, on the Irish Sea.

Brunel was ambitious. In 1839 he built the *Great Britain* which was two and a half times as big as the *Great Western*. Even that was not enough. In 1859 he launched the *Great Eastern* which was 19,000 tonnes. She gave Brunel so much work and worry that he became seriously ill. However, he was sure his ship would be a success and he lay in bed waiting to hear good news of her maiden voyage. Instead, he was told that a violent explosion had blown off one of her funnels, and done a lot of other damage. Brunel had faced his problems with great courage all his life, but this was too much. Within a few days he was dead.

the *Great Eastern*

Brunel's work was far from wasted, though. In the early days, when the crew of a sailing ship saw a steamer, they used to jeer at the 'puffing kettle'. Sometimes they trailed a rope over their stern, suggesting the steamer needed a tow. After Brunel, though, it was clear that one day steamers would take the trade of the world from sailing ships.

Work Section

Understand Your Work

1 Transport in the Early Eighteenth Century

1 Why did many people in the early eighteenth century not worry if their roads were poor?
2 Who was in charge of the roads in each village? How was he chosen?
3 How did a) poor people b) richer people, have to help look after the roads?
4 What was the main problem in road building? Give two ways in which it might be solved?
5 How were stage coaches built? Why?
6 What was the only way for people to travel quickly?
7 Give two ways of carrying goods by land. What disadvantages were there with each?
8 What was the best way to move heavy goods?
9 What vessel did the Severn boatmen use? Name four ways of driving it.
10 Why did London need a lot of coal? Where did it come from? How was it carried?

2 Turnpike Roads

1 What problem did the village of Stanton have? What did Parliament allow the villagers to do?
2 When did other villages begin to have the same problem as Stanton?
3 Who, usually, formed a Turnpike Trust? How did a Turnpike Trust a) collect its money b) spend it?
4 How many Turnpike Trusts were there by 1830?
5 Why did Turnpike Trusts employ proper surveyors?
6 How did Telford build roads? Which was his most famous road? Name a bridge he built.
7 How did Macadam build roads?
8 Whom did Macadam employ to break stones? How did they work?
9 How were coaches improved? How fast could they go?
10 What services did coaching inns give? Which of these services was the most important?

3 Canals

1 What problems did the Duke of Bridgewater have with his mines, and the transport of his coal? How did he think he could solve these problems?
2 What was known about canal building? Why did the Duke think James Brindley could help?
3 What was built at Barton? Why?
4 How did the Bridgewater Canal help the people of Manchester?
5 Where did Josiah Wedgwood want a canal? Why?
6 Who built the Grand Trunk Canal? How long was it? How many locks and aqueducts did it have? What was there at Harecastle?
7 What shows that canal building was dangerous?
8 At what time were many canals built? What was their most important cargo?

9 What problems were there with a) boatmen b) canal boats c) the canals themselves.
10 What advantages did canals have over roads?

4 Early Railways and Locomotives

1 Who built the first waggon ways? How were they made?
2 How were waggon ways kept as level as possible?
3 Name three ways of moving waggons.
4 Where were there many waggon ways? What use were they?
5 How were rails improved? When?
6 Who made a steam locomotive that ran on the road? Who made the first steam locomotive to run on rails?
7 Who wanted to build a railway from Stockton to Darlington? Who engineered the line?
8 What drew the trains on the Stockton and Darlington line?
9 What gauge was the line? How was it decided?
10 Who disliked the railway? Why? Why did most people welcome it?

5 The Liverpool and Manchester Railway

1 When was the Liverpool and Manchester line opened? Who was killed at the official opening?
2 Who had decided to build the railway? Why?
3 Who was the engineer?
4 Who objected to the line? Why?
5 How did they try to stop the work?
6 Why was a tunnel built at Liverpool?
7 How was the railway carried over Chat Moss?
8 Why did the Directors hold the Rainhill Trials?
9 Which locomotive won? Who had built her?
10 What happened when the Liverpool and Manchester line was seen to be a success?

6 Sailing Ships

1 What things about a clipper ship show she was built for speed?
2 How were ships of the eighteenth century built? What famous company owned a fleet of ships?
3 Who designed the first clipper? When?
4 Why did shipowners reject his design at first?
5 What two things made them change their minds?
6 Which country first had clipper ships?
7 Who built the first successful British clipper?
8 Why were British clippers better than their rivals?
9 Why was life on a clipper a) dangerous b) unpleasant?
10 Why did clippers race from China to England? Who were the two leading ships in 1866?

7 Steam Ships

1 Why did Isambard Brunel suggest building the *Great Western*?
2 Name a bridge and a railway built by Brunel.
3 How many steamships were there in Britain by 1830? What work did they do?

4 Why was it impossible for one of the early steamships to cross the Atlantic? What was Brunel's answer to the problem?

5 When and where was the *Great Western* launched? Why was she taken to the Thames?

6 What ship beat her in the race across the Atlantic?

7 What proved that the *Great Western* was the better ship?

8 Why was building the *Great Eastern* very ambitious?

9 Why did Brunel die?

10 Why was Brunel's work with steamships important?

Use Your Imagination

1 You are a farmer who has been chosen Surveyor of Highways for your village. Describe a day's work on the roads. (1)

2 Write a report on the problems of navigation on the River Severn. (1)

3 You are an inhabitant of Stanton. Write a letter to Parliament, asking permission to set up a toll gate. (2)

4 Draw up a list of rules John Macadam might have made for road builders. (2)

5 Imagine you are the Duke of Bridgewater in his old age. Tell the story of your canal, and say why it was important in the history of transport. (3)

6 It is 1790. Decide where you would like a canal in your area. Write an article for a newspaper to persuade people to support your plan. (3)

7 You are a mine owner in County Durham. Write the story of a waggon way you built for your pit. (4)

8 You are a locomotive on the Stockton and Darlington line. Describe a day in your life. (4)

9 You have a good view of the opening of the Liverpool and Manchester railway. Describe what is happening to a friend who cannot see. (5)

10 You have made your first journey by railway along the Liverpool and Manchester line. Say what you think will be the future of railways in Great Britain. (5)

11 You are John Griffith. Write a letter to a ship owner asking him to let you design a clipper for him. (6)

12 You are a sailor on a clipper ship. Make a list of the things your ship owner and captain should do to make your life easier. (6)

13 It is 1835 and you are Isambard Brunel. Say how you see the future of the steamship. (7)

14 You are the ship *Sirius*. Write the story of your life. (7)

15 What were the most important improvements which took place in transport between 1700 and 1750?

Further Work

1 Look for remains of turnpike roads in your area. Toll houses and coaching inns are quite common. Ask about local turnpikes at your library.

2 Draw a diagram to show the time taken to travel from London to Edinburgh:
   a before turnpikes.
   b on the turnpike roads.
   c by rail today.

3 Study a map of the canal network of Great Britain. Where were most canals built? Can you think why?

4 What canals were built in your area? If there were none, try and discover why.

5 Find out more about William Murdoch and Richard Trevithick.

6 What famous locomotives, not mentioned in this book, were built before 1830?

7 Find out what you can about the history of your local railway.

8 Read more about life on board a sailing ship, for example, in R. H. Dana's *Two Years Before the Mast*.

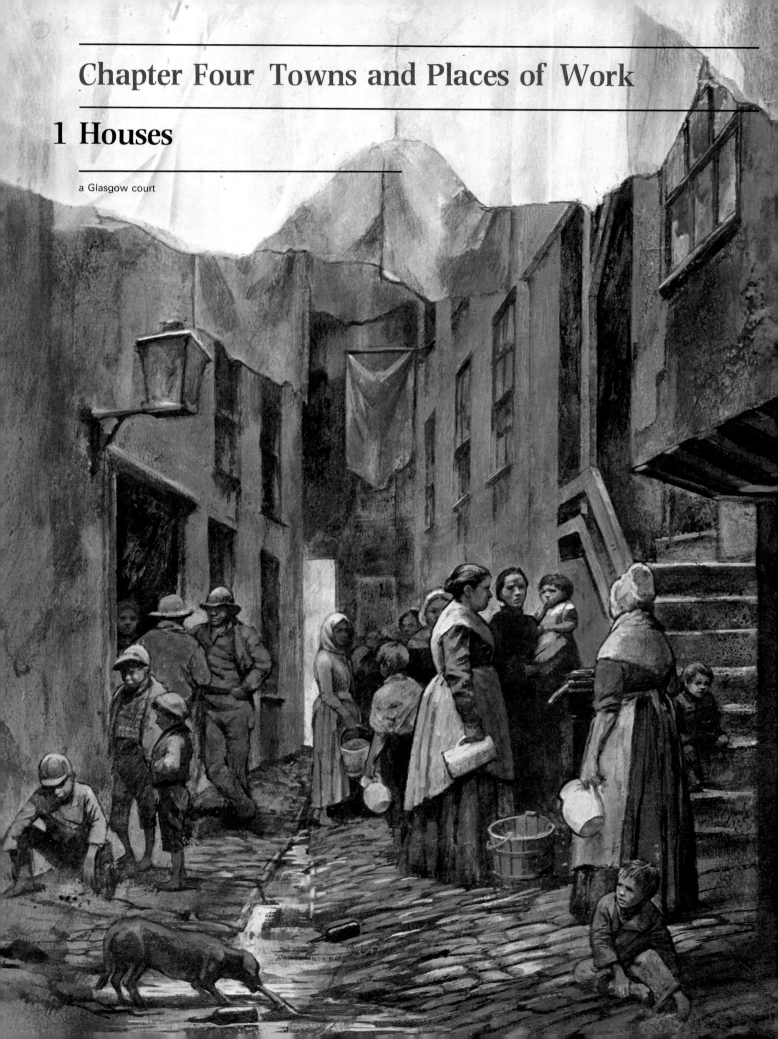

Chapter Four Towns and Places of Work

1 Houses

a Glasgow court

1 Houses

The previous picture shows you some houses that poor people lived in over a hundred years ago. It is in Glasgow, but it could have been in London, Birmingham, Liverpool or any large city. We are standing in what they called a court. Ahead, we can see an entrance which is not much bigger than a doorway, but behind us the end of the court is open, so that it is just possible for a cart to come in to collect rubbish. The people hang their washing on poles stuck from their windows, because they have no gardens. Next to this court is another, then another, and another. There are shopping streets in a different part of the town, full of people and horse-drawn vehicles of all kinds, making a tremendous clatter on the stones. This, though, is where the poor live, and this is where they will return, men, women, and children, after a hard day's work. They will have little energy for amusing themselves in the evenings, and on Sunday when they might have enjoyed some fresh air, there is nowhere to go. The countryside is too far away for them to walk, and there are no parks. All they can do is lounge around the court, gossiping, quarrelling and fighting, or else, if they have a little money, drinking in a public house.

If we visit one of these houses, we step straight into the living room. The first thing we notice is the smell for, if all the family are at home, the room will be crowded with people. None of them wash a great deal, and they are so afraid of fresh air that they stop every crack they can find, and stuff rags into any broken windows. The floor is brick – cold, hard and dusty. The builder has done nothing to make the house waterproof so the walls are black with damp. There is a coal fire burning, but that is more for cooking than for keeping the room warm. The children have to take turns to sit by it. The family keep their coal and their food in the same cupboard under the stairs. The furniture is a plain table, with some hard chairs, and some beds with grubby mattresses, full of bugs. Several share the same bed and some sleep under it. The family live, cook, eat and sleep all in the same room, so it is not surprising that they go drinking whenever they can.

The stairs lead directly out of the room to the ones above it. The family cannot use the extra rooms, though, for they have let them to lodgers.

If we could go into the attic we would see how badly the roof is made, with thin timbers, and signs of leaks. Some windows will not open, and some of the doors will not stay shut on their own. It is no use looking for a kitchen or a bathroom, since the house has neither, and the lavatories, which all the neighbours share, are outside, at the end of the court.

Like the rooms upstairs, the cellar is let to lodgers. Only the poorest will rent a cellar, for it is a dreadful place to live. It may have a fireplace, but no window, or, at best, only one at street level. As the family is poor, they cannot afford furniture and sleep on straw. The walls and floor are always damp, and water pours in after heavy rain. In the worst cellars the people have to take the door off its hinges and lay it on bricks, if they are to have somewhere at all dry to sit. In Liverpool there were many cellar dwellings that were so bad that the town council ordered the people living in them to leave, and filled the cellars with earth. It was not long, though, before the landlords had dug them out and let them to poor Irish families.

Not many places have underground sewers, but instead, deep, open drains called 'kennels' (channels). There is a kennel in the middle of the court in the picture. Not only rain water, but all the waste water from the houses runs in them, so they are most unpleasant. The barefooted urchins who live in the court do not mind, though, and jump in and out of them quite happily.

They call their lavatories 'privies', which means 'private places', but in fact they are very public because, usually, the whole court has to share one. A privy is a deep, brick-lined cess pit, with a wooden seat on top. When the cess pit is full, men are supposed to come and empty it. They make such a smell that they are only allowed to work at night, so they are called 'night men'. Often the privy overflows and the filth finds its way into the cellars.

On the left of the picture you can see the stand pipe from which they all draw their water. The water companies only turn it on once a day for about half an hour, so at that time there is always a crowd of people round the tap, arguing, pushing and trying to fill their tubs and buckets. Nor is the water pleasant, for the company takes it from the nearest river, which is where the town's sewage is dumped. One man who thought his water was tasting particularly nasty, took off his tap and found in the pipe the decayed body of an eel.

4 Prisons

What happened to John Ray, the man who was brought before John Fielding? He was sentenced to be hanged, but, as usually happened, the punishment was changed to transportation. He was taken to Barbados, in the West Indies, where he worked as a slave on a sugar plantation. He was supposed to stay there for ten years, but the heat and the hard work killed him quite soon. One of John's friends who had been caught with him was flogged, and another was branded on the hand with a red-hot iron. In the eighteenth century it was unusual to send a criminal to prison. Most prisons were for debtors.

We will visit the Fleet Prison in London. Just inside the gate is a yard full of people – men, women and children. Some are enjoying themselves with a game that looks a bit like tennis, others are playing skittles, and the rest are sitting about, gossiping. There is a lot of noise from a room in one of the buildings, and, looking in, we see it is a bar, with people drinking, laughing and shouting.

A prisoner tells us his story. 'I used to be a ship-owner, but I lost nearly all my vessels. A few were wrecked, but most, the French took. I borrowed money and, in the end, owed £20,000. My creditors had me locked in here, but it will not do them any good. I will never be able to repay them.

Luckily, my parents are rich enough to send me money, so I live quite well. You can buy anything in prison that you can outside. It's just that the jailer takes his profit, so you pay a lot more. I have a couple of rooms, which means my wife and children can live with me. They are allowed to go in and out of prison as they like, and I can have friends to visit me. Sometimes I long to take a walk in the park, or go up the river in a boat, and it's miserable to think I may die in this place. Still, on the whole, life could be a lot worse.' *'But what happens if your parents stop sending money?'* 'Oh, I would hate to be a poor debtor. This is the masters' side. It is quite different on the common side, where the poor are. They are locked up together, and only come into their yard once in a while. They are filthy, and they have to live on bread and water. The jailer doesn't like them, because he can't make any money out of them. A while back, he chained one of them to a dead body, until a friend paid his admission fees.' *'Admission fees?'* 'Oh, yes, you have to pay to come in here, even though you are an unwilling visitor.'

A hundred years later, prisons were quite different. We will visit Pentonville, which was built in 1842. It is for criminals only, since debtors are no longer sent to prison. The governor shows us round. 'In the old days, no-one bothered much about criminals. They used to hang them, flog them, or send them overseas. We still send some to Australia, but more and more are going to prison, and we try and make better men of them. It isn't easy. The main thing is that we stop them speaking to each other. When a man is out of his cell, he must wear a mask, but most of the time, he is locked up on his own. We call it solitary confinement. It is wonderful what it will do. When they come in, some of them are big, boasting bullies. They swear and shout in their cells for a time, but after a few weeks on their own, they quieten down. I saw our chaplain talking to one this morning. The big thug was crying like a baby. The chaplain says he can make them think good thoughts, but I don't know.'

We follow the governor down one of the wings of the prison. Everywhere is spotlessly clean. From some cells comes a 'latitat' noise, and from others, a tapping noise. Prisoners are either weaving or shoemaking. Suddenly, a bell booms out, and warders move quickly from cell to cell, unlocking the doors. The convicts stream out, their heavy boots clanging on the iron galleries and stairs. Each one wears his mask, and they do not speak. They go into the prison chapel, where every man has his own cubicle, and cannot see his neighbours. The chaplain conducts a short service, and the men join in with good will. Probably, it is the only chance they will have of using their voices today. 'They have an hour's exercise in the yard, as well as chapel,' says the governor, 'but the rest of the time they are in their cells.' *'What happens if any of them misbehave?'* The governor shows us a punishment cell. It is completely dark, and completely silent. 'Bread and water and a few days in there will tame anyone,' says the governor.

5 Schools

We will now follow a child from one of the slum houses to school. His name is Alfred, and he is five years old. His parents only send him to school because they are at work all day. There is no law to say children must attend school, and as soon as he is eight or nine, Alfred will have to go to work himself.

Since it is Monday, Alfred takes twopence (1p) with him. That is his school fee for the week. All but the poorest children have to pay fees. Alfred's parents think they are worth paying in order to be rid of him. The rest of the money the school needs is given by the wealthier people in the town. They hope the school will teach the children religion, so that they will grow up into honest, law-abiding citizens. Apart from paying a little towards the salaries of the teachers, the government gives no help at all.

The school is just one big, gloomy room. The windows are high up, so the children cannot look out of them. The walls are stone, with no plaster. The floor is worn and dusty. The only heating is a brick stove. The children who sit near it are too hot, and the fumes make them cough, but most of the room is cold.

Alfred's first lesson is religion. The clergyman has come to take it himself. He has all the children, about sixty of them, and he tries to teach them their Catechism. The children stumble over the hard words. They can make no sense of them, and some begin to fidget and talk. The clergyman loses his temper. He tells them about hell fire and says that people who are wicked will burn for ever after they are dead. Alfred understands that well enough, and is very frightened. He often has bad dreams about hell.

After the clergyman has gone, Alfred has a writing lesson. He sits with his friends on an uncomfortable bench, and in front of them is a long tray, filled with sand. The children trace letters in the sand with their fingers. 'A', shouts the teacher, so they all try to draw a big, capital A. When they have it right, they smooth the sand. They then go to B, and so on through the alphabet. Older children have slates. They are supposed to clean them with damp sponges, but most use 'spit and shirt cuff'. Only the oldest have pen and paper. Some of them write beautifully. They do not write their own ideas, though. Most of the time they are just copying sentences from a book.

After writing, they have reading. The children stand in small groups round reading sheets. First comes the alphabet, next there are words of two letters, then words of three letters, and so on. In the end, they have sentences taken from the Bible. The oldest children read the Bible itself, though sometimes, as a rare treat, they are given a story book.

The only other subject is arithmetic. The younger children chant their tables, and the older ones do problems. Sometimes they work on their slates, but the master is fond of making them do difficult sums in their heads.

Alfred's teacher is only ten years old. He is one of the older boys in the school, who has been made a

monitor. He has to come to school every morning, one hour before the rest. The master tells him what he must teach Alfred and his friends during the day. Often he does not understand the work himself. Alfred learns little from him. The school has several monitors, each one with a class of ten.

In the school, there are also two pupil teachers. One is fifteen and the other is seventeen. Both became pupil teachers at fourteen. They teach all day in the school, and in the evening the master gives them lessons. They have to learn subjects like English, history and geography, and they have to pass an examinnation at the end of each year. If they do well, they go to a training college for teachers, when they are eighteen or nineteen.

The only adult in the school is the master. He has a difficult time. He has to teach his monitors every morning, and his pupil teachers every evening. Also, the school day is long. The children do not wash, and they are badly behaved. There is always a noise, because everyone is trying to work in the same room. The master often gives the cane, but he has some unusual punishments as well. Sometimes he ties a child in a sack. He also has a basket, with a rope and a pulley. If a boy is especially naughty, he puts him in the basket and hauls him up to the ceiling.

6 Factory and Workshop

In the last section you saw that only the youngest children went to school. As soon as they were about nine years old, their parents sent them to work. We will see what happens to a boy called Mark, who works in Mr. Orrell's cotton factory.

Mark has a long walk to the factory. He has to leave home at 5.00 in the morning to arrive on time. His house is like the ones on page 66-7. Compared with home, the factory is a palace. It is well built, with an iron framework and brick walls. Mr. Orrell keeps the rooms at the same temperature all the year round. This is important for the cotton. Mark likes it as well, for he is neither cold in winter, nor too hot in summer. In Mark's home parents and children are on top of each other, but in the factory there is plenty of space. There is a fresh air, too, most of the time. Even in winter Mr. Orrell says the windows must be open a little. The work people often shut them, however, because they do not like draughts. The factory is light, for there are plenty of windows, and after dark they have gas jets.

Mark does not like his work. He is a 'scavenger', and helps look after the mules. The cotton makes a lot of dust, which Mark has to sweep up. He must go everywhere in the room, even under the machines. They do not stop the machines for him, so he needs to be very careful. There have been some dreadful accidents. Once, a boy caught his arm in the machinery, Another time, a girl put her head too close to one of the big driving belts. The buckle caught her hair, swinging her up to the ceiling and over the pulley.

Mark's job is not hard, but it is boring. Some days he has to spend fourteen hours just brushing up dust. The spinners, that is, the men who operate the mules, are quite kind. They have to see the children do their work, though. At the end of a long day, Mark is sleepy, so his spinner keeps him awake by twisting his ears. Sometimes, he hits him with his belt, which is against Mr. Orrell's rules. If Mr. Orrell sees people doing wrong, he fines them. One day the overlooker caught Mark giving his friend a ride on his back. It was stupid and dangerous. At the end of the week, Mark found he had lost sixpence ($2\frac{1}{2}$p) from his wages. As he only earns 1/6 ($7\frac{1}{2}$p), that was a lot for him. His father beat him, because he always takes Mark's wages.

In Wolverhampton there is quite a different factory, belonging to a man called Hemingsley. Here they make iron washers. Mr. Hemingsley employs about fifty children including Anne Preston.

Anne is fifteen, but is small for her age. Her dress is no better than a piece of sacking. Her arms and head stick out through holes, making her look like a tortoise. She is very dirty. Anne cannot remember either of her parents. She was brought up in the workhouse, and still lives there because she has no home.

Anne has to be at the factory at seven in the morning. At nine o'clock she stops work for half an hour to have breakfast, and she has an hour for dinner, from one o'clock until two o'clock. After that, though, she has to work without stopping until 8 o'clock. Her only free day in the week is Sunday. Her wages are 4/- a week.

Mr. Hemingsley's factory is in a dreadful state. It's floors are so rotten they have to be held up with props, and its walls are cracked. None the less, it is full of heavy machines, so the whole building is shaking and groaning. One day a floor did collapse, killing several people, and it is likely to happen again.

We follow Anne into the factory. The noise is overpowering. We have to walk very carefully because the machines are close together. We could easily lose an arm if we fell into one of them. Anne has to work with two wheels whirring round a few inches either side of her head. In front of her a heavy hammer crashes down every two seconds. She has to feed it small pieces of metal, so that it stamps them into shape. If she is a little bit careless, the hammer will come down on her hand.

Mr. Hemingsley could easily box in the working parts of his machines, and put little guards in front of the hammers to keep the children's fingers from going under them. However, that would cost him money, so he will not do it. 'It isn't often they lose a hand', he explains. 'The machine just takes off the top of a finger. Anyway, they should watch what they are doing. It's just carelessness on their part – sheer carelessness.'

We will now go to Sedgley, near Birmingham. Here we meet George Brown, who is a nailmaker. George does not go to a factory, but helps his father make nails at home. They have a little workshop behind the house, where the whole family work together. It is a hut, about the size of a small bedroom. The walls are thin and the roof leaks. The floor is dug out, all round the edge of the room, and the family stand in this ditch. They use the centre of the room as a work bench. On it they put their tools, and in the middle is a coke fire. It fills the room with choking fumes.

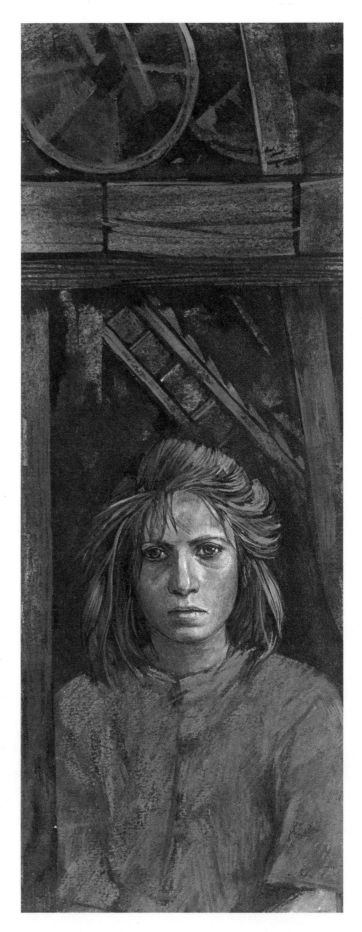

Factory and Workshop

Every week a man delivers some long, thin bars of iron. The family heat the metal in the fire, then beat it into shape with hammers. The hut is full of noise, it is very hot, and everyone is crowded together. They are often cross with each other. George's father sometimes loses his temper. Once, he hit his daughter with a red-hot bar. Another time, he sent George what the people of Sedgley call a 'flash of lightning'. When a bar of iron comes out of the fire, it is covered with little bits of red-hot coke. The way to be rid of them is to shake them on the floor. What George's father did, was to shake them all over his son. They fell in his hair, on his face, and inside his shirt. They covered his body with tiny burns.

George's father can work when he likes, and his wife and children have to keep the same hours that he does. He takes Sunday as a holiday, and he usually spends most of Monday in bed. With a lot of grumbling he does some work on Tuesday afternoon. On Wednesday he may work for much of the day. On Thursday he is a worried man. All the iron must be made into nails by Saturday evening, and there are only three days left. Mr. Brown gets up at six, and drags his wife and children into the workshop. There they stay, hammering as hard as they can, for sixteen hours. Mr. Brown keeps them awake by shouting at them, and hitting them. Before he goes to bed, George has to make 1,000 nails.

When he collects the money for the nails, Mr. Brown keeps it all himself.

7 Coal Mines

Today will be exciting, for we are going to visit a coal mine in County Durham. Mr. Hudson will be our guide. He is a viewer, which is a kind of foreman.

While we are waiting at the top of the pit, Mr. Hudson shows us two steam engines. They are wheezing and banging away. 'This one is the pumping engine,' says Mr. Hudson. 'It pumps 70,000 gallons of water out of the pit every hour. It is a Newcomen engine. It has been here for a hundred years and still works well. The other is the winding engine, which means it lifts the coal out of the pit. It is a later design, by Boulton and Watt. Some pits still use a horse capstan to wind their coal, but we mine 800 tons a day. A horse could never lift all that. Well, here is our bucket now.'

The winding engine has drawn a huge, empty bucket to the surface. We get in rather nervously, and suddenly begin to drop. After a while we do not feel as if we are falling, but the hole at the top of the pit becomes smaller and smaller. In the end, it looks just like a star in the sky. After four minutes, there is a clanking noise, and the bucket stops. We get out, to find ourselves in a dark, damp tunnel, which they call a 'gate'.

'It is a mile to the coal face,' says Mr. Hudson. We go along the tunnel which, at first, is lined with bricks, and is quite high. After a while, though, we have to stoop. There are no bricks and we see loose stones in the roof. We cover the last part of the journey crawling on our hands and knees in dirty water. Everywhere, we are in a strong draught. From time to time we go through a door, and the air makes it bang behind us.

At last we reach the coal face. Here one of the hewers explains how he digs the coal. 'First I take my pickaxe and I cut a slot in the bottom of the seam, about three feet deep. That weakens it, you see. Next, I drive some wedges into the coal, and down it falls. All I have to do then is to shovel it into the corves. My wife and my two boys take them to the pit bottom.' These corves are big baskets, on wheels.

One of the boys describes his work. 'I am a hurrier, and I have to hurry, too. Father is paid for every corve he sends to the surface, and if I don't carry the coal fast enough, he beats me. In these narrow workings I have to drag the corve.' He shows us a belt he is wearing, with a chain. 'I hook the end of the chain to the corve, and pull it. In the main gates, though, there are rails, so I can go quite fast. I get behind the corve and push with my hands and head.' The little boy lifts his lamp to show us a bald patch right on top of his head.

'Coal mining must be dangerous, Mr. Hudson.' 'We have a lot of accidents. Most are because of the men's stupidity. I saw some the other day, smoking in a part of the mine where we have a lot of gas. Once, the engine boy did not stop the winding engine in

time, and drew a bucket with six men over the pulley. Several fell back down the shaft. Some accidents they can't help. A few years back, one of the gates collapsed, and some people were trapped. By the time we had dug through to them, they were dead. Most of our accidents, though, come from the odd rock falling out of the roof.' *'Do you have explosions?'* 'We take great care about that. They can be nasty. One near here blew twenty men out of the pit. It shot a great beam through the air like an arrow and it stuck in the side of a hill. Our men have safety lamps. We also ventilate the mine pretty well. There are two shafts, an upcast and a downcast. Under the upcast shaft we have a furnace. It draws air right through the workings. The doors make sure the air goes to all parts of the pit, otherwise it would take short cuts.' At each of the doors there is a little child, about five years old. We ask one of them what his work is. 'I am a trapper. When the hurriers come by with their corves, I have to open my door for them.' Mr. Hudson says, 'I am sorry for the little trappers. They sit in the dark, and the hurriers frighten them with tales of hobgoblins.'

We ride up the shaft and get out at the top, relieved that we have landed safely. *'One last question, Mr. Hudson, where does your coal go?'* 'We have a horse railway that carries it to the River Tyne, about twelve miles away. Then it goes by collier brig down to London. London people would be very miserable without Durham coal to keep them warm.'

Work Section

Understand Your Work

1 Houses
1 What are the two entrances to a court?
2 How do people who live in a court spend their spare time?
3 Why are there unpleasant smells in the house?
4 Why does the family find home uncomfortable?
5 What is wrong with the way the house is built?
6 What rooms do you have in your own house that are not found here?
7 Why were cellar dwellings uncomfortable and unhealthy?
8 What is a kennel? What takes its place today?
9 Why were privies unpleasant and unhealthy?
10 What was wrong with the water supply?

2 Disease
1 Where did cholera come from? What are its symptoms? How is it spread?
2 What are the symptoms of typhus? How is it spread?
3 Who was most likely to catch smallpox? How did it affect them?
4 What disease killed most people? What were its symptoms?
5 How did doctors explain disease?
6 Give two reasons why patients often died as a result of operations.
7 What happened about typhus, cholera and tuberculosis?
8 Who discovered how to prevent smallpox? What was his method?
9 When was the Board of Health set up? What two things did the Board encourage local councils to provide?
10 Why did some people oppose the Board of Health? What seemed unreasonable about this opposition?

3 Police
1 How were constables chosen? Why was the job unpopular? What were the duties of a constable?
2 Why were watchmen inefficient?
3 How were ordinary people encouraged to arrest criminals? Why did few of them do so?
4 Where was John Fielding's house? For what purpose did he use it?
5 What were Bow Street Runners? Name three ways they made money.
6 Who started the Metropolitan Police? When?
7 Who were the two Commissioners of the Metropolitan Police? How did they organise their force?
8 Describe a constable in the Metropolitan Police.
9 What crimes were the Metropolitan Police able to control? How?
10 Why did the Commissioners of the Metropolitan Police not employ many detectives?

4 Prisons
1 What usually happened to criminals sentenced to death in the eighteenth century?
2 What other ways were there of punishing criminals?
3 Who were most of the people in prison in the eighteenth century?
4 Why was life pleasant enough for a rich prisoner?
5 How did poor prisoners suffer?
6 What was the main aim of a prison in the nineteenth century?
7 How did they try to achieve this aim at Pentonville?
8 What work did the Pentonville convicts do?
9 How were convicts prevented from speaking to each other?
10 What happened to a convict if he misbehaved?

5 Schools
1 At what age did children normally leave school?
2 Why do wealthy people give money to the school? Name two other ways in which the schools found money.
3 In what ways is the school room unpleasant and uncomfortable?
4 Who takes the lesson in religion?
5 On what do the children write apart from paper? Why is it, do you suppose, that only the oldest children have paper?
6 What do the younger children read? What do the older ones read?
7 What do the children learn in arithmetic?
8 What seems to be the most important subject?
9 What is a monitor? What is a pupil teacher?
10 Why does the master have a difficult time?

6 Factory and Workshop
1 In what ways is Mr. Orrell's factory more comfortable than Mark's home?
2 What is a 'scavenger' in a cotton factory?
3 What accidents may happen to factory children?
4 Why does Mark dislike his work?
5 In what ways are factory children punished?
6 Describe the building in which nails are made.
7 Who makes the nails? Why is the work unpleasant?
8 How does Mr. Brown sometimes punish his children?
9 Why was Mr. Brown's working week bad for his children?
10 Which is the more unpleasant place for a child to be – the cotton factory or the nailmakers' workshop? Why?

7 Coal Mines
1 What work does the Newcomen engine do at the pit?
2 What work does the Boulton and Watt engine do? What was the old method?
3 How far is it from the pit bottom to the coal face?
4 What tools does a hewer have? How does he use them?
5 What work does a hurrier do?
6 What accidents can happen in a coal mine? Which is the most common?
7 Name two things done to prevent explosions.
8 Why are there doors in the pit?
9 What is the work of a trapper?
10 How is coal transported from the pit? Where does most Durham coal go?

Use Your Imagination

1 Draw up a list of rules you think house builders of the nineteenth century should have followed. (1)
2 Your friend is ill in bed in one of the houses on page 66. You sit by the window and tell him what happens through the day. Write what you say. (1)
3 You have been sent to stay in one of the houses described in Section 1. Write a letter to your parents asking them to have you back home at once. (1)
4 You have visited a hospital in the early nineteenth century. Describe what you have seen. (2)
5 If you suddenly found yourself living in 1830, what precautions would you take in order to stay healthy? (2)
6 You are living in Marylebone in 1750. Explain why you would like a proper police force in your area. (3)
7 Write a story about an eighteenth-century criminal. (3, 4)
8 You are in the Fleet Prison. Write a letter to a friend asking for money. Explain why you need it. (4)
9 You have just served a sentence in Pentonville Prison. Explain why you do not intend to commit any more crimes. (4)
10 Alfred describes his day at school to his mother. Write what he says. (5)
11 Imagine we could bring Alfred alive today. What would he say if he spent a day at your school? (5)
12 Draw up an Act which you think Parliament should have passed for the protection of child workers. (6, 7)
13 Three children meet and talk about their work. One works in a cotton mill, one down a mine, and one makes nails. Write what they say. (6, 7)
14 You are a child of twelve, living in 1830. Write the story of your life. (All)
15 In what ways do you think children today have a better life than those of the early nineteenth century? Children, today, commit more crimes. Can you suggest why that is?

Further Work

1 Find out more about Edwin Chadwick and the Public Health Movement.
2 Find out more about the Seventh Earl of Shaftesbury.
3 Who discovered a) anaesthetics b) antiseptics?
4 Read about the eighteenth-century criminal, Jonathan Wild.
5 Find out why watchmen were called 'Charleys'.
6 Find out more about nineteenth-century prisons, e.g. the use of the crank and the treadwheel.
7 Read about the work Joseph Lancaster and Andrew Bell did for schools.
8 What did the Education Act of 1870 say?
9 Find out how Parliament eventually protected children a) in textile factories b) in coal mines.
10 You can learn a lot about the way people lived in the nineteenth century from novels written at the time. Here are a few suggestions:

Conditions in towns	Dickens, Charles. *Bleak House*, Chapters 16, 22 and 46. Kingsley, Charles. *Alton Locke*, Chapter 35.
A hospital	Dickens, Charles. *Sketches by Boz*, Chapter 6.
Typhus	Gaskell, Elizabeth. *Mary Barton*, Chapter 6.
Working conditions	Kingsley, Charles. *Alton Locke*, Chapters 2 and 8.
A school	Dickens, Charles. *Our Mutual Friend*, Book Two, Chapter 1.
A prison	Dickens, Charles. *Great Expectations*, Chapter 39.

Chapter Five   Britain and North America

1 Canada

To start with, in this chapter, we are going to visit some of the settlers in North America, in the eighteenth century. We will begin our journey in Canada, which belongs to France.

Early in the sixteenth century, fishermen from Brittany began sailing to the rich fishing grounds off Newfoundland. They said there were so many cod, that all they had to do was lower baskets into the sea, and pull them out, full of fish. Later, other Frenchmen wanted to go further. They hoped that they might find treasure, as the Spaniards had done in Mexico. In fact, there was no gold or silver, but they did discover wealth of another kind. In those days, it was the fashion to wear tall, wide-brimmed hats made of felt, and the best felt came from beaver fur. Beavers were common in Canada, so people found they could make a lot of money from trapping. Frenchmen began to settle along the banks of the St. Lawrence. In 1608 Samuel de Champlain built a little settlement which grew into the city of Quebec, and in 1662 the Sieur de Maisonneuve founded Montreal. These were the two most important towns in New France.

Each year, there was a fur fair at Montreal. Traders came from all over Canada, bringing goods the Indians wanted – axes, knives, kettles, blankets, ornaments and brandy. The Indians came too, in a great fleet of about 500 canoes laden with beaver pelts. The trading usually began quietly enough, but in the evening the Indians drank the white man's 'fire water'. They stripped naked and raced through the streets, whooping, screaming and waving their tomahawks. The inhabitants closed their shutters, barricaded their doors, and longed for the fair to end.

By the early eighteenth century there were perhaps 50,000 people in New France. The most important were the seigneurs, or gentry. Each one had been given land by the King, and all he had to do in return was to clear it and encourage settlers. Some seigneurs lived in log cabins, being no richer than ordinary farmers, but others were wealthy. One of them, Charles le Moyne, built himself a fortified house of stone just like a castle in France. It was surrounded by a high wall, two hundred feet by one hundred and seventy, with towers on the corners.

The seigneurs let their land to farmers, called 'habitants'. Each year the habitant had to pay his seigneur a rent of a small amount of money, along with some of his produce, such as wheat and live

a habitant's farm

chickens. A farm began on the river bank, which was important for transport. Next, came level, fertile land for grazing, and growing crops. At the far end was forest, where the habitant found timber for his buildings and fuel for the long, cold winter. The piece of land was perhaps two hundred yards wide and over a mile in length. Farms were long and narrow, because that way everyone could have his share of river bank, fertile soil, and forest.

The farmhouse was built of logs, with an earth floor. There was just one room, with a loft above it, where the children slept.

The habitants were honest and hardworking, but their lives were dull. A young man who wanted adventure became a 'coureur de bois'. This means, literally, 'a runner in the woods'. He would vanish into the forests for perhaps eighteen months or even four years. He might be killed by a grizzly bear or, much more likely, by Red Indians. His biggest problem, though, was to stay alive during the terrible Canadian winter. Many coureurs de bois were better hunters than the Indians, and even made better birch bark canoes. These men went into the forests to trap beavers, not just for adventure. They came home when they had enough pelts, but their dangers were not over. What they had done was against the law, and if the authorities caught them, they had them whipped and branded.

Jesuit missionaries had even more courage than the coureurs de bois. Any normal person, however brave, avoided hostile Indians when he could. Jesuits looked for them deliberately, hoping they could convert them to Christianity. Indians often tortured their prisoners to death, and could be especially cruel to 'Black Gowns', as they called the priests. Even the thought of dying horribly did not dismay the Jesuits. 'The blood of the martyrs', they said, 'is the seed of the Church.'

One Jesuit, Isaac Jogues, fell into the hands of the most terrible enemies the French had, the Iroquois Indians. They tortured him until he was badly maimed, when some Dutchmen, who were allies of the Iroquois, helped him escape. He went home to France, where he could have stayed, but he insisted on returning to Canada. He found that someone was needed to go on a mission to the Iroquois, and since he could speak their language, he volunteered. On his way he met fugitives who said the Iroquois were on the warpath, but he would not turn back. Again, the Indians tortured him, and this time they killed him.

a hunter

2 New England

We will now leave the French in Canada, and sail down the east coast of the continent, to Boston, in Massachusetts. The people are English. Indeed, this part of America is called New England.

The first settlers here were the Pilgrim Fathers, who arrived in 1620. They were strict Puritans. These were people who thought the Church of England had a great many faults, and wanted to 'purify' it. The government persecuted them, so they decided to go to America, where they would be free to worship as they pleased. Their ship, the *Mayflower*, arrived at Cape Cod, a rocky headland in Massachusetts Bay. Here they made their homes. Soon other Puritans arrived. They built the town of Boston, and settlers pushed inland, in spite of the Red Indians.

As the sea was full of cod, many New Englanders became fishermen. There were plenty of forests, too, so others were shipbuilders. Numbers of them were merchants, trading with Europe and the rest of America. First, we will meet a fisherman, who will tell us about his work.

'I have a schooner, with a crew of six men. We fish for cod on the Grand Banks, near Newfoundland. The round trip is about a thousand miles, but we go there and back three times in a good season.

'To catch the fish, we go over the side of the schooner in our dories. These are little rowing boats. Each man has a long line, with hooks. He baits these with bits of mackerel. The cod are greedy, and will swallow the bait readily enough. If I have done my

fishing for cod

job properly, and found a good shoal, the men are soon rowing back to the schooner with their dories full. The trouble with fish is that it goes bad quickly. We have to split the cod, throw away their insides and heads, and then drop them in barrels of brine. As soon as our barrels are full, we come back home to Boston. Here we spread the fish to dry. When that is done, we call it "stockfish". Stockfish will keep for a long time, even on a sea voyage to Europe, or the West Indies.

'It is fishermen like me that have made New England rich. The cod is the emblem of Massachusetts, so you can see how important he is for us.'

Now we will call on a merchant, Paul Green. He lives in a handsome house in a fashionable street. He has the best quality carpets, elaborate mahogany furniture, and gold and silver table ware. Mr. Green looks like a rich London merchant. His street and his house, too, could well be in London. 'How do you make your money, Mr. Green?' 'I trade with Europe and the southern colonies. I send tons of stockfish to Spain and Portugal. The inhabitants of those Popish countries eat it because of their religion. The British buy masts and spars for their ships. Our pine trees are just right for that. Then we have a lot of beaver fur from the Indians, up in the mountains, and we send that to Britain as well. In the southern colonies they have slaves, whose owners are glad to have our stockfish to feed them. We also send them horses and, from time to time, a little corn. They sell us sugar, rum and tobacco, as well as hardwoods for our furniture.

'I prosper because I am a man of God. They have dancing these days in Boston, and folk even play with cards – the Devil's picture book. I waste no time on these things. I spend twelve or fourteen hours every day, in my counting house, save on Sunday. That is a day for prayer.'

Mr. Green is a stern father. He will not let his children play games, and on Sunday he takes them to the Meeting House. The preacher often gives a sermon that lasts for two hours. The children must listen carefully, the whole time, without fidgeting or whispering. Mr. Green is superstitious as well as religious. He is terrified of witches. At Salem, in 1692, it was men like him who had twenty wretches hanged for witchcraft. He is something of a hypocrite, too. He hates the Roman Catholic Church, and he thinks that slavery is wrong. However, he is quite happy to trade with Roman Catholics and slave owners. In fact, most of his money comes from them. But he is very honest in his business, and is hardworking. It is such men who have made Boston one of the richest towns in America.

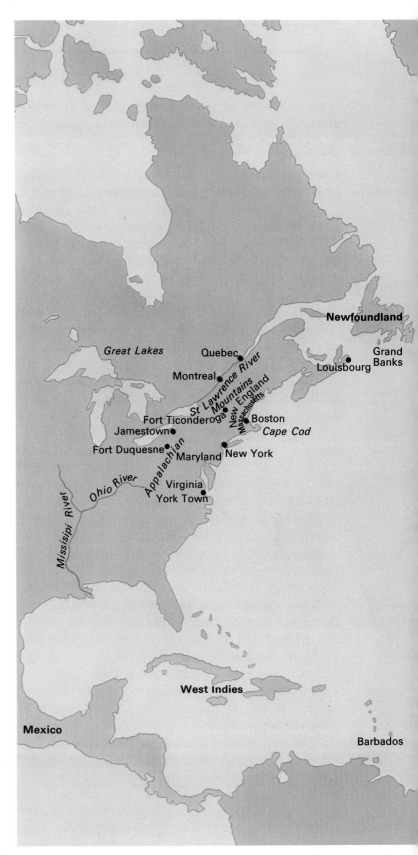

the eastern part of North America

3 Virginia and Barbados

Leaving Boston, we sail over 400 miles south, to Virginia. This was the first English colony in America. Sir Walter Raleigh had hoped to discover gold and silver, as the Spaniards had done. In the reign of Queen Elizabeth, he sent two lots of settlers here. The first group went home in despair, and the second vanished. Then, in 1607, some twenty years later, the ship *Susan Constant* brought 105 immigrants, who built a fort at Jamestown. They did not behave very sensibly. For example, when they wanted firewood, they tore down their homes, rather than do the harder work of felling trees. After two years only 38 of them were still alive. They packed, and set sail for home. At the mouth of the river, though, they met a ship bringing supplies and more settlers. They plucked up courage and returned.

Gradually, the new colony began to prosper. The settlers found no gold or silver, but they did discover a crop that was to make them richer than silver mines would ever have done. It was tobacco. The first Europeans in America were amazed to see Indians smoking, and even more so to find they could go for several days without food, as long as they had their tobacco. There was a Spanish doctor who thought tobacco could cure all sorts of complaints – rheumatism, toothache, headache, stomach-ache, chilblains, snake bites and wounds. James I of England, on the other hand, disliked smoking so much that he wrote a book called *A Counterblast to Tobacco*. In it he said that the body of a man who smoked a lot would be full of soot, like a chimney. People found tobacco very satisfying, though, and took no notice of the King. They not only smoked it, but also chewed it, brewed tea with it, and turned it into snuff. Virginians were soon making a lot of money growing and selling tobacco. In their own country it was so important that they used it for money, instead of coins.

The seed was sown in the spring, and all the time the plants were growing, slaves had to hoe the soil and pick caterpillars from the leaves. In the autumn, the leaves began to turn colour. That meant it was time to pick them, and hang them in bundles to cure. When the tobacco was ready, they packed it into huge barrels weighing half a ton. They rolled these down to the ships. Planters whose land was a little way from the water had to make special tracks called 'rolling roads'.

The planters were rich. Some of them owned thousands of acres of land, and lived in mansions, like the big country houses in England. They were very different from the poor habitants of New France. They were also very different from the Boston merchants, for they were no puritans. They left all the hard work to their slaves, while they enjoyed themselves. They squandered their money on luxurious furniture, clothes and carriages, they kept many servants, and they gave expensive parties. For all their large incomes many were deeply in debt, something which would have horrified a strict Bostonian.

Our last port of call is the island of Barbados, in the West Indies. Here, too, the inhabitants made themselves rich, and again, it was not from gold and silver. This time it was sugar.

The first Europeans to arrive were Spaniards, but all they did was to take away the natives to work in the silver mines on the mainland. Some English settlers arrived in 1625, and found the island deserted. Within a few years, they started to grow sugar cane. This was hard work, especially cutting the cane in the hot sun, so they bought negro slaves. After they had cut the cane, they crushed it between rollers to squeeze out the liquid. The rollers were driven by windmills. There were several hundred of these on the island. Next, they boiled the liquid to take out the sugar. This was a long, complicated job, lasting several months. As well as sugar, they produced a sticky treacle called molasses, and molasses could be made into rum. Sugar and rum were two luxuries for which the people in Europe paid high prices. The planters in Barbados became rich. Like the tobacco planters in Virginia, they lived in magnificent houses, with expensive furniture. They had expensive tastes as well, and often spent more money than they could afford.

The main town of Barbados, Bridgewater, was well built. The island had good roads made from broken coral. There were plenty of forts, with heavy cannon, to keep away the French and the Spaniards. Barbados is only thirty miles long, and twenty wide, so it is smaller than an English county. None the less, the people of Great Britain looked on it as their most valuable colony.

From just the few visits we have made, we can see how important North America had become to European people. In the north, the seas gave fish, and the forests, furs and timber. From the hot lands further south came luxuries like tobacco, sugar and rum. All this was worth fighting for, and there were some bitter wars.

4 The Slave Trade

You have seen in the last two sections that the planters in Virginia and Barbados used Negro slaves. This was true of all the English colonies south of Maryland, and in all the West Indies.

⁎ One of these slaves will tell us his story. He is from the Ibo tribe in Nigeria. 'My home used to be deep inside Africa. We had a hard life, but at least we were free. One day, a gang of black men attacked our village. We fought as best we could, but they had firearms and they soon overpowered us. They destroyed ten villages in our region, and took many prisoners. They put heavy collars round our necks and tied us in long lines. They then made us walk many miles every day.

They struck us with whips if we did not walk fast enough, but every so often someone would fall exhausted. They just shot him where he lay. We could not understand where they were taking us, but we were sure we were going to be eaten.

'At last we reached the sea. Here, I saw my first white men. They had red faces, straight, loose hair and they wore strange clothes. With them, they had bales of cloth, iron axes, iron pots, and some of those terrible firearms that had so frightened us when our village was attacked. They looked at each one of us carefully, prodding and poking, and they argued a lot with the black men who had captured us. Then I realized what was happening. We were being sold. ⁎

'We spent a few days locked in dungeons in a fort. Other captives joined us, from different tribes. My wife and children were taken from me, and I never saw them again. I was put with strangers, and we could not speak each other's languages.

'Then came the worst five weeks of my life. We were taken to a ship, chained together, and packed into the hold. The heat and the smell were unbearable. Many died from disease, and some just from despair. Each day the sailors collected a few more dead bodies and flung them over the side. One day, a number of people broke loose and jumped into the sea. I tried to kill myself by not eating, but some sailors forced my mouth open with a piece of iron, and made me take food. We still had no idea where we were going, but we were sure that there was a horrible death waiting for us at the end of our journey.

The Slave Trade

'At last the voyage ended, and we were more terrified than ever. We were taken to a market place, where we were sold once again. My new master brought me here. He did not kill and eat me. He whipped me once, when I disobeyed him, but most of the time he is anxious to keep me in good health. He treats me rather as he does his horse, and for much the same reason. He wants me to work. I have to toil for long hours in the heat of the sun. Cutting the sugar cane is especially hard.

'I have a new wife, but she is one my master chose, and I do not like her. We live in a little one-roomed hut, with wooden walls and a mud floor. Our food is mainly corn and salted fish. We dip the fish in flour, boil it, and then add hot peppers to give it some flavour. On Sundays, our master lets us rest. We dance and sing together and tell our children the stories that we learnt in Africa. Their favourites are the Anansi tales, about a man who was also a spider.

'Sometimes we talk of rebelling against our masters, and sailing back to Africa. We know in our hearts, though, that it can never be. We are going to be slaves, and so will our children and our children's children for ever more.'

No-one knows how many Africans were taken to America as slaves, but at least two million went to the British colonies alone. In 1700 they were sold for £15 each, on average, and by the 1750s they fetched £40. There was a lot of money to be made. Merchants in Liverpool and Bristol loaded their ships with cotton cloth and iron goods. They exchanged these for slaves in Africa, and sold the slaves either in the West Indies or in the southern colonies on the mainland. With the money they bought sugar or tobacco. The ships went out, then, with common, cheap goods, and came home with valuable luxuries. Men in the slave trade became rich, as did the planters.

After a time, though, more and more people saw how wicked the slave trade was. Men like Thomas Folwell Buxton and William Wilberforce spent years trying to persuade Parliament to make it illegal. Parliament finally did so in 1807.

5 The British Conquer Canada

As we have seen, both France and Britain had colonies in North America. Each wanted to take the vast areas of land that remained. The British were hemmed in by the Appalachian mountains, and the French tried to hem them in even more. They built forts along the Mississippi and around the Great Lakes. Then, in 1753, they built Fort Duquesne in the valley of the Ohio. This annoyed the Virginians, who felt their enemies were coming far too close. They sent a force of militia, under Major George Washington, to drive them away. The French defeated Washington, as well as a British army under General Braddock, which came out later.

The war now began in earnest. However, there was fighting in Europe as well, and the French King was worried about his enemies in Germany. He only sent 3,500 men to Canada. On the other hand, the British Prime Minister, William Pitt, was determined to conquer North America. He sent 20,000 troops, and there were 22,000 colonial volunteers as well. Also, the British navy was there to help the army. The French only held on as long as they did, because they fought bravely, and because they had an excellent general, the Marquis de Montcalm.

Since he was heavily outnumbered, Montcalm fought on the defensive. In 1758 he defeated a powerful British force that attacked Fort Ticonderoga. However, the British army, helped by the navy, captured Louisbourg near the mouth of the St. Lawrence. Then, early in 1859, Montcalm decided he must concentrate his forces so he abandoned both Fort Ticonderoga and Fort Duquesne. Everything now depended on the defence of Quebec.

In June 1759, a British fleet of 50 warships and 120 troop transports anchored off the Isle of Orleans, near Quebec. They had been five weeks nosing their way up the St. Lawrence River. In charge was General James Wolfe. He was tall, but lanky, with sloping shoulders and he had a double chin. Also, he was young for a general, being only thirty-two. His appearance was misleading. Though he certainly did not look it, he was a man of great determination, and a brilliant soldier. He was going to need all his courage and skill.

Quebec stands on a headland, with cliffs facing the river, so it was impossible to attack it directly. Down-

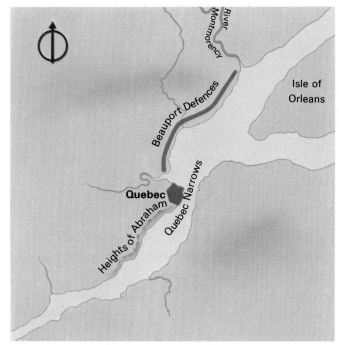

the attack on Quebec

stream, there were the strong Beauport Defences. As for going upstream, it seemed impossible to take ships through the Quebec Narrows, with their strong currents. Wolfe thought his best plan was to force the Beauport Defences. He landed his army by the River Montmorency, and attacked again and again. One day he lost 400 men in just two minutes. The French stood firm, and as the weeks passed, the British began to despair. By early August, Wolfe was ill and in bed. Then, in late August, he ordered his troops to abandon their camp by the River Montmorency and go to the south bank of the St. Lawrence. The French were delighted, for they were sure they were winning.

Wolfe, however, was not leaving. A British warship, the *Sutherland*, had sailed through the Quebec Narrows, showing it was possible to attack Quebec from the other side. However, the river bank was easy to defend, for there were cliffs all along it. Montcalm put groups of 50 men at likely places, and sent 1,000 of his best troops under Colonel Bougainville to patrol the area. The small groups would be able to hold off any landing party until Bougainville came to their aid.

the death of Montcalm

Wolfe decided the only way was to cross secretly in the dead of night. At 2 a.m. on September 13th, nearly 2,000 men rowed ashore, using muffled oars, and in complete silence. A sentry challenged them, but a Scottish officer knew enough French to answer him. The leading men made their way up the steep face of the cliff and took the small French force at the top completely by surprise. Wolfe then ferried over more and more men, and when dawn broke, Montcalm was horrified to find 4,500 of his enemies on the Heights of Abraham, just outside the town. He had as many men himself, though, and he led them out to give battle.

The French advanced firing and shouting as they came. Wolfe's men lay down until the last minute, when they stood in line and waited in silence. The French came on, still firing and shouting. When they were only fifty yards away the British soldiers fired a tremendous volley. That was all that was needed. The one volley smashed the French army to pieces, and the survivors turned and fled.

The battle lasted only ten minutes, but when it was over Quebec was taken and soon afterwards, the whole of Canada. Many brave men died, though, on both sides. Among them were General Wolfe and General Montcalm.

The British Conquer Canada

the death of General Wolfe

6 The American War of Independence Begins

During the conquest of Canada, Britain and her thirteen American colonies fought side by side against the French. A few years later they were fighting each other. Why was that?

A New England merchant will tell us what he feels about Britain. 'The British look on the American colonies as their back yard. We produce all sorts of things Europeans need – furs, timber, fish and tobacco. We want the best prices for our goods, but can we sell them where we like? Oh no! We have to send everything to Britain. Well, we need manufactured goods. Out in the New England countryside, for example, they want muskets, iron ploughs, knives, hoes and hundreds of thousands of nails to build their log cabins. Can we buy these things where they are cheapest? Not at all. We have to buy from Britain.' *'Can't you make them yourselves?'* 'The British will not allow it, otherwise we would have a flourishing iron industry in New England.

'Another thing, we fought the French to stop them taking the land beyond the Appalachians. There are thousands of square miles out there, inhabited by a handful of Indians. We need that land badly, and once we had beaten the French, we thought we could move into it. But what do the British say? They say that all territory west of the Appalachians is crown property, and we cannot take an inch of it.

'The worst thing, though, is their taxes. A while back, they suddenly decided that every legal document and newspaper must have a revenue stamp on it. Well, we put a stop to that. We burnt all the stamps, and one stamp master had to ride so fast to escape the mob, that his horse died under him. Then they tried taxing our imports, like cottons, wines and silks. We just refused to buy those things.' *'But everyone has to pay taxes!'* 'I know, but only if they agree. No-one is going to tax me without my consent, and all good Americans feel the same.' Now let us hear what the British Prime Minister, Lord North, has to say. 'Of all the ungrateful rascals in the world, the Americans must be the worst. They were in mortal danger from the French and the Indians, until we saved them. It cost us millions of pounds, and the lives of thousands of our soldiers. When we asked them to help us, all they said was, "We will come if you will pay our expenses." In the end we had to give them £1 million to fight for their own homes.

'Well, we decided that if the Americans did so little during the war, they could at least help when it was over. Their trade is useful to us. We need their goods and they need ours. What better to exchange with one another, rather than with our enemies? Then they have a long frontier to defend – some 2,000 miles. There are still some French settlements beyond it, as well as many hostile Indian tribes. That frontier has to be defended. We gave them a full year to make some suggestions, hoping they might raise an army of their own. They said nothing. "Very well," we told them, "we will look after the frontier, but you must help pay." We imposed some very light taxes, but they were so angry and vicious that we had to remove most of them.

'The main problem is that we have conquered Canada. The Americans are no longer afraid of the French. They think they do not need our help any more, so they are not bothered how much they annoy us.'

the Boston Tea Party

The troubles in America became really serious in 1773. The government tried another tax, this time on tea. Two hundred men from Boston decided to do something dramatic. Dressed as Red Indians, they boarded three ships in the harbour. They then poured £18,000 worth of tea into the sea. They called what happened the Boston Tea Party.

The British government was furious, and closed the port of Boston, so that there could be no more trade there. It was a savage punishment, and the Americans were furious in their turn. All the colonies sent delegates to what they called a Continental Congress. It was a kind of parliament. You probably know that Congress still meets today to make laws for the American people. The Americans prepared to fight, too. The young men formed armed companies. They called themselves Minute Men, because they were ready to fight at a minute's notice. Also, the colonists collected secret stores of weapons and supplies.

In 1774, the governor of Boston heard there was an arms store at Concord, eighteen miles away, so he sent a small force to destroy it. American spies heard of his plan, though, and a Boston silversmith called Paul Revere rode through the night, calling the Minute Men to arms. In the morning, they tried to stop the British at Lexington. The British scattered them, and went on to destroy the arms dump at Concord. They then went back to Boston, with the Americans firing at them from every rock and tree. The Americans lost eight men at Lexington, but their snipers killed nearly 300 British on their return march. The war had begun.

the battle of Lexington

7 The Americans Win Their Independence

George Washington

At the beginning of the war, there were plenty of Americans with fine words to say. One of their orators, Patrick Henry, exclaimed, 'Give me liberty or give me death.' When Thomas Jefferson wrote the Declaration of Independence in 1776 he included this famous statement:

'We hold these truths to be self evident, that all men are created equal, that they are endowed by their Creator with certain inalienable Rights, that among these are Life, Liberty and the pursuit of Happiness. That to secure these rights, Governments are instituted among men, deriving their just powers from the consent of the Governed.' Many of the men who signed this document owned slaves!

Congress issued the Declaration on July 4th, which the people of the United States still celebrate as Independence Day. The first congressman to sign, John Hancock, wrote his name large and clear, saying that King George III must be able to read it without his spectacles.

So much for fine words, but when it came to fighting the rebel Americans did not do very well. All sorts of men joined the army. There were farmers, lawyers, labourers and criminals. All were hard to discipline. A German officer who tried to help them complained that he had to give the reason for every order before his men would obey. Their Commander in Chief, George Washington, said in despair, 'Never was such a rabble dignified by the name of army.' British regular soldiers, on the other hand, were the best in the world. In an open battle, they were almost sure to win. For example, at Guilford Courthouse in 1781, a British force of 1,900 beat 4,500 Americans. Most of the rebels fired one shot and ran.

A big problem was that Congress found it hard to raise money. The American taxpayer was as mean during the war as he had been before it. In the winter of 1777 Washington's army was camped at Valley Forge. They were in rags, dying of disease, and living on 'a leg of nothing and no turnips'. When Washington asked Congress for supplies, they told him to plunder the local farmers. Washington refused.

Why, then, did Britain lose the war?

In the first place, Congress chose the right man to be Commander in Chief. As we have seen, he was George Washington. Washington was a planter and slave owner from Virginia. He was not a brilliant general, but he was brave and determined. He thought that if he could hold on long enough, he might one day have the chance to win a great victory, and end the war.

Secondly, though they were not much good in battle, many of the rebels were splendid guerrilla fighters. Lots of them were frontiersmen who were excellent marksmen. They had been shooting wild animals and Red Indians all their lives.

Thirdly, the American colonies covered a vast area. The British had only a few thousand troops, and though they might win battles they could not hold the land they conquered. The best they could do was to occupy the most important towns on the coast, like New York. Here, they were fairly safe, as long as they had the Royal Navy to help them.

Most important of all, though, the Americans found allies. The French wanted revenge for the loss of Canada, but they did not wish to lose another war. Then, in 1777, a British general, John Burgoyne, blundered into the forests of New England. He was surrounded by a much larger force of Americans, and had to surrender at Saratoga. He lost 6,000 men, which was bad enough. What was far worse, his defeat encouraged the French to help the Americans. Soon afterwards Holland and Spain joined them. Britain was on her own. Her enemies attacked her colonies in the Far East, they attacked her islands in the West Indies, and the Spaniards besieged Gibraltar. There was even talk of invading Britain herself.

the battle of Bunker Hill

French money, French supplies and French soldiers poured across the Atlantic. Even more important, the Americans now had a powerful navy on their side. Washington saw that if the French would attack places like New York from the sea, while his army attacked from the land, the British could be defeated. Twice Washington tried to persuade the French to help in this way, and failed. Then, in 1781, he heard that the French Admiral de Grasse was going to Chesapeake Bay. Here, General Cornwallis had a force of 7,000 men in Yorktown. After six years of waiting, Washington's chance had come. He marched as fast as he could to Yorktown.

the British land troops in New York

Cornwallis found himself besieged by an army of 16,000 French and Americans, while there were twenty-four French warships out in the bay. He fought as long as he could, but, in the end, he had to surrender. His men laid down their arms and marched out of the town. As they did so, their band played an old tune, 'The World Turned Upside Down.'

Yorktown need not have been the end of the war, for a few months later Admirals Rodney and Hood smashed the French fleet at the Battle of the Saints, in the West Indies. However, Yorktown made it seem the war might drag on for years. The British were tired of fighting, so in 1783 they made peace, giving the thirteen colonies their freedom. They became the United States of America.

Work Section

Understand Your Work

1 Canada
1 Which Frenchmen first came to Canada?
2 What did others who came later hope to find? What, in fact, did they discover?
3 Name two Canadian cities and the men who founded them.
4 Where was the annual fur fair held? What happened at the fair?
5 Who were the 'seigneurs'? Who had given them their land?
6 Who were the 'habitants'?
7 Why were farms laid out in long, thin strips?
8 What was a 'coureur de bois'?
9 Why did Jesuits look for Indians?
10 Which tribe was the most dangerous?

2 New England
1 Which settlers first arrived in New England? Why did they go there?
2 What important town was built on Massachusetts Bay?
3 What fishing ground do New Englanders visit?
4 What method of fishing do they use?
5 How do they preserve their catch?
6 What shows that Paul Green is prosperous?
7 With which countries does he trade?
8 What goods does he handle?
9 What shows that Mr. Green is very religious?
10 What people does he fear? What people does he dislike?

3 Virginia and Barbados
1 Who first tried to start a colony in Virginia? Why?
2 When was the first permanent settlement founded?
3 What crop did the Virginians find profitable?
4 How was it cultivated?
5 How were the Virginian planters different from the Boston merchants?
6 What happened to the natives of Barbados?
7 When did the first English settlers arrive?
8 Name two goods which Barbados exported?
9 Why was Barbados heavily fortified?
10 Why did European countries fight over North America?

4 The British Conquer Canada
1 What land did both Britain and France covet?
2 Where had the French built forts? Where did they build Fort Duquesne?
3 What happened as a result of the building of Fort Duquesne?
4 Why did Montcalm fight a defensive war?
5 What victory did Montcalm have in 1758? What successes did the British have?
6 What decision did Montcalm make in 1759?
7 When did Wolfe besiege Quebec? Where did he make his first attack?
8 Explain how Wolfe was able to take his army to the Heights of Abraham.

9 Why did the British win the Battle of Quebec?
10 What was the result of the capture of Quebec?

5 The Slave Trade
1 Which colonies used slaves?
2 Who captured the slaves in the first place? How were they taken to the coast?
3 What happened to the slaves when they reached the coast? Why do you suppose slaves from different tribes were mixed together?
4 Why did many slaves die on the voyage to America?
5 What work did slaves have to do? Where did they live? What did they eat?
6 How did slaves keep alive their memories of Africa?
7 How many slaves were taken to the British colonies in all?
8 What goods did slave ships take to Africa? What goods did they bring back from America?
9 Why was the slave trade profitable?
10 Name two men who opposed the slave trade. When was it made illegal?

6 The American War of Independence Begins
1 In what ways did Britain control the trade and industry of her colonies?
2 What did the Americans hope would happen after the conquest of Canada? Why were they disappointed?
3 What taxes did the British impose? Why did the Americans object to being taxed?
4 What complaint did the British have about the way the Americans behaved during the war against the French?
5 What excuse did the British make for controlling the trade of their colonies?
6 Why did the British government tax the Americans?
7 Why were the Americans not worried about annoying the British after the conquest of Canada?
8 What happened at Boston in 1773?
9 How did the British government punish the people of Boston? How did the Americans react?
10 Explain why there was a battle at Lexington in 1774. What happened as a result of the battle?

7 The Americans Win Their Freedom
1 Who wrote the Declaration of Independence? When did Congress issue it?
2 Why was the American army not very efficient?
3 What problems did Washington have at Valley Forge?
4 What qualities did Washington have? How did he hope he might win the war?
5 At what kind of fighting were some of the Americans very good?
6 Why could the British do little more than hold the larger ports?

7 Why did the French want to help the Americans? What encouraged them to do so? What other countries attacked Britain?

8 How did Washington hope the French navy would help?

9 Why were the British defeated at Yorktown?

10 Why did the loss of Yorktown bring the war to an end?

Further Work

1 Write a story about a coureur de bois. (1)

2 You are a seigneur who wants some settlers to come and live on his Canadian estate. Write an advertisement for a French newspaper. (1)

3 Write a report on Boston and its trade for the British government. (2)

4 You are one of Paul Green's children. Write about your home and your father. (2)

5 You are a Virginian planter. Describe your estate, your home, and the life you lead. (3)

6 You are a slave trader. Write a letter to a friend persuading him to invest some money in your business. (4)

7 Write a speech to persuade Parliament to abolish the slave trade. (4)

8 You are General Montcalm. The British have just arrived to besiege Quebec. Explain how the war has gone until now. What plans do you have for the defence of Quebec? (5)

9 Make a running commentary on the battle on the Heights of Abraham. (5)

10 How do you think the British could have prevented the American War of Independence? (6)

11 Summarise the arguments put forward by the New England merchant and by Lord North. With which side do you agree? (6)

12 Write a story about an American soldier during the War of Independence. (6, 7)

13 You are a British soldier fighting the Americans. Write a letter home describing your experiences. (7)

14 You are George Washington. The French have just entered the war on the side of the Americans. Say what problems you have had, and how you think the French will be able to help. (7)

15 It is 1770. Write an article for a newspaper explaining why it is important for Britain to control as much of North America as possible. (All)

Use Your Imagination

1 Read about some of the French explorers in North America, e.g. Cartier, Champlain and La Salle.

2 Read about the Iroquois Indians and their wars with the French.

3 Find what you can about William Penn and Pennsylvania.

4 Read Kipling's *Captains Courageous*. Though written much later, it will give you a good picture of cod fishing on the Grand Banks.

5 Read more about the early settlers in Virginia. Who was Pocahontas?

6 You have seen that the slave *trade* was made illegal in 1807. When was slavery itself abolished a) in the British colonies b) in the United States?

7 Read more about the battles fought during the American War of Independence.

8 What do the stars and the stripes mean on the American flag? When was the 'Stars and Stripes' first flown?

9 Read more about George Washington. What did he become after the War of Independence?

10 Many Americans remained loyal to Britain during the War of Independence. What happened to them after the war?

Chapter Six   The War Against Napoleon

1 France Under Napoleon

It is 1812. We will go to Paris to visit Monsieur Lebois, who is a banker. He has a handsome house in a brand new street called the Rue de Rivoli. His furniture is expensive, with a great deal of rich, gold ornament. The walls are hung with silk, while the emblem of the eagle is everywhere. The eagle reminds us that France is ruled by an Emperor, Napoleon Bonaparte.

Both Monsieur Lebois and his wife are small, round, plump and very rich, *'You have a fine house, Monsieur.'* 'It was not always so. We have had a terrible time in France.' *'What happened?'* 'It all began in 1789. The King, Louis XVI, was desperate for money, so he asked the Estates-General* to meet and help him rule the country. We were all pleased, because we thought that at last bankers, merchants, and other people like myself were going to have a say in the government. Until then, it was just the King and nobles who counted. The only time they had any use for us was when they wanted to borrow money. It all went wrong, though.' *'Why was that?'* 'It was the leaders of the Paris mob, the Jacobins, who seized control, not respectable citizens at all. The mob was completely out of hand.' 'They *were* starving,' says Madame Lebois. 'That may be, but there was no need to behave as they did. First they tore down the Bastille,** and then the executions began. I could hardly feel sorry for the King and the nobles when they lost their heads. Before long, though, they were killing quite ordinary people – anyone they thought might be an enemy. The tumbrils used to rattle

* They were a bit like the British Parliament.
** A royal fortress, like the Tower of London.

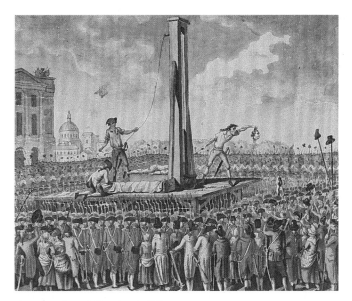

the execution of King Louis XVI

through the streets taking the victims to the scaffold. The guillotine was busy all the time. My wife and I went to see it one day, but once was enough. We knew our own turn might come quite soon.' Monsieur Lebois's double chin quivers at the thought.

'That wasn't all,' Madame Lebois goes on. 'These men, the Jacobins, plunged us into war with the whole of Europe. Austria and Prussia attacked us by land, and Great Britain by sea. At one time we thought Paris itself would fall.' *'How did it all end?'* 'We were saved by Napoleon,' replies Monsieur Lebois. 'He became a great general, and then used his position to make himself Emperor. He was crowned in 1804. He has done wonders for France. We now have gold coins in our pockets. It just used to be worthless, paper notes. There is plenty of trade and industry, so my bank is doing well. France now has the best secondary schools in the world. We have a new code of laws as well.' 'Think of the improvements to Paris,' says Madame Lebois. 'We have gas lighting in the streets, pure, fresh drinking water in the homes, and there are all the marvellous new buildings, like our street, the Rue de Rivoli. The Emperor has even thought of a new way of numbering houses – even numbers down one side, and odd numbers down the other. It makes finding an address so easy. I like the Opera, too. There were no entertainments during the Revolution, but Napoleon himself enjoys the Opera. We have seen him there several times with his new Empress. He is especially fond of Italian music. He is Corsican, you see, so he is practically an Italian himself.'

'He gave us back our Sunday, too,' says Monsieur Lebois. *'What do you mean?'* 'My wife and I are Catholics, but no-one was allowed to go to church during the Revolution. They even crucified some peasants in La Vendée, because they refused to pull down a cross. The churches are open again now.' *'So you have no complaints about Napoleon?'* Monsieur and Madame Lebois look at each other uneasily, and then Monsieur Lebois says, 'Well, we do not like the war. It seems the Emperor wants to rule the world. He hates the British, but he can't conquer them, because their navy is too strong. There is a dreadful war against the Spaniards. If those people capture a French soldier, they torture him to death. Now, Napoleon has invaded Russia.'

Tears come to Madame's eyes. 'Our only son, François, is an officer in the Imperial Guard,' she says. 'It is a great honour, but we would rather he was at home, helping in the bank. Just now, he is with the army, on the way to Moscow. We do not know if we will ever see him again.'

2 The British Navy

When France declared war on Great Britain in 1793, her army was many times larger than our own. All that stopped a French invasion was the British Navy. It was enough. Admiral Jervis said proudly, 'I don't say the French can't come: I say they can't come by sea.'

the *Victory* under full sail

Today, one of the old battleships, H.M.S. *Victory*, is in Portsmouth Harbour. She is 227 feet long and weighs 3,500 tonnes. You can compare this with a modern aircraft carrier, which may be 900 feet long and weigh 50,000 tonnes. A battleship was a floating fortress. *Victory* carried 100 guns, which were on three decks, as you can see from the picture. They are nearly all at the side. In battle, a ship fired her guns, one after the other, very quickly, so it was like a roll of thunder. This was called 'firing a broadside'. The weakest part of a ship was her stern, because the officers' cabins were there, and they had glass windows. The best position was to have your broadside to your enemy's stern. Then, you could fire all your guns into her and she could reply only with a few. Some of your shot might go the whole length of the other vessel and do terrible damage. This was called 'raking' an enemy.

Victory at the time of Trafalgar

1 Mizzenmast   2 Quarter Deck   3 Mainmast   4 Fo'c'sle
5 Foremast   6 Upper Gun Deck   7 Nelson's Day Cabin
8 Nelson's Sleeping Cabin with his cot   9 Middle Gun Deck
10 Wardroom   11 Entry Port   12 Lower Gun Deck   13 Orlop
14 Sick Bay   15 Midshipman's Berth — here Nelson died
16 Powder Room   17 Shot Locker

The British Navy

What was it like to be a sailor? A midshipman called Edward Power will teach us. *'How old are you Edward?'* 'I am twelve.' *'That is young to go to sea.'* 'Not at all. There are many midshipmen younger than I am. We want to be officers as soon as possible, so we start young. I hope to be a lieutenant by the time I am eighteen. The ordinary sailors are grown men, of course. Sometimes, I have to command a boat's crew. The men don't like taking orders from a boy, but they have to do as I say. It's not often that I give orders, though. I have lessons from the school-master, and the officers teach me how to manage the ship. Also, I am Lieutenant Jones's servant. I have to look after his cabin and clean his equipment. If he is not pleased with me, he sends me to the masthead.' Edward points to a small platform, high in the rigging. 'You can imagine what it's like to stay up there for three hours in a gale. Still, that's not as bad as the punishments the men have. They are flogged with the cat o'nine tails. One was hanged, even, last year.'

Next, we talk to one of the seamen, George Evans. 'I am a master gunner. I have three men to help me. To load our gun we first ram in a bag of gunpowder, and after it, a wad, to hold it tight. Then we put in the shot. Next, my mate lays the gun. That means he points it at the correct angle. We fire when ordered. As the gun goes off, it leaps backwards, so we have to be well to one side of it. Before reloading, we swab out the barrel with a damp sponge, to make sure there are no sparks left. We have to be quick, because the enemy will not wait for us. *Victory* can fire three broadsides

the battle of the Nile

in under four minutes. If an enemy ship gets all three, she is finished. We always fire into their hulls. The French, they fire into our rigging, hoping we won't be able to chase them.' *'How did you join the navy, George?'* 'I used to work on a collier brig, so I was a good sailor. I volunteered to get away from my wife. Lots of the crew, though, were taken by the press

gang. Many a man has been out walking, had a crack on the head, and woken up on this ship. Once on board, you don't leave until the war is over. I have been five years on "Victory". None of us likes it. There is danger from shipwreck, or having an arm or a leg shot off by the French. If we are at sea for a long time, all we have to eat is salt beef and ship's biscuits. Discipline can be hard. Nelson is a good man – strict but fair. On some ships the officers enjoy having the men flogged. What bothers us most, though, is our pay. We only have nineteen shillings a month, and mostly it is in arrears.'

This, then, was how Britain treated the men whom she expected to save her from the French. It is not surprising that in 1797 there was a mutiny in the fleet. The sailors wanted all sorts of things, but mainly more pay. As the government was expecting a French invasion at any time, it at once raised the pay of the ordinary seaman to twenty-nine shillings a month. The King also gave a royal pardon to everyone who had taken part in the mutiny. Most of the sailors went back to their duties willingly enough.

111

3 The Battle of Trafalgar

Napoleon won many battles, and by 1803 he had only one important enemy left. That was Britain. He determined to conquer her, so he gathered a large army at Boulogne. From there, on a clear day, he could see the white cliffs of Dover. He could have taken his soldiers across quite easily if it had not been for the Royal Navy. He said, 'Let us be masters of the Straits for six hours, and we will be masters of the world.'

The French had a good navy, but it was scattered. There were ships in Brest, Rochefort, and Toulon. Spain, who was France's ally, had ships in Ferrol and Cadiz. Outside each of these ports was a British fleet, blockading it. Napoleon's plan was that the French should escape from their harbours and sail to the West Indies. That would frighten the British, because their West Indian islands were important for their trade. Doubtless, the British would send a large fleet to defend them, much as you would rush to protect your money box if someone was after it. When the French ships met, they were to hurry back across the Atlantic and seize control of the English Channel. With any luck, Napoleon's soldiers could invade England before the British fleet returned from the West Indies.

At first, Napoleon's plans went well. The French Admiral at Toulon was Villeneuve, and the English Admiral blockading him was Nelson. Nelson allowed Villeneuve to escape and then wasted time hunting for him in the Mediterranean. Villeneuve, though, headed across the Atlantic, and it was some weeks before Nelson realised where he had gone. He then chased after him. None of the other French squadrons joined Villeneuve, so he came back to Europe. He hoped he might help his friends escape and join with him to sail up the Channel. What happened though, was that he met a British fleet under Admiral Calder, off Cape Finisterre. Calder drove him away, so he went to Cadiz, where he joined the Spaniards. He now had a fleet of thirty-four French and Spanish ships, but in the meantime, Nelson had returned. He was off Cadiz with twenty-nine British ships. What was Villeneuve to do? He decided to come out and fight.

The French Admiral drew up his ships in line of battle. He thought the British would form a line of battle, too, and fight broadside to broadside. His gunners would fire at their enemies' rigging, so that his ships could escape quite easily, if they wanted. Nelson was determined they should not. He divided his fleet

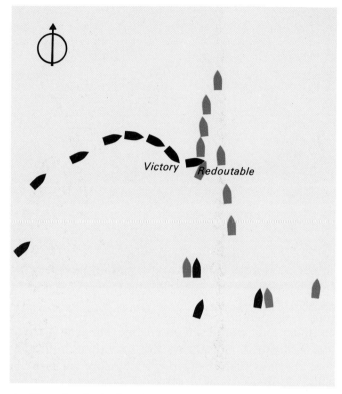

the *Victory* breaks the French line

into two. One part he commanded himself. He put it in line behind his flagship *Victory*, and cut the enemy fleet in half. He engaged the middle of their line and the wind made it difficult for their leading ships to join the battle. Meanwhile, Admiral Collingwood with the other half of the British fleet destroyed the remaining third of the enemy. Nelson ordered his captains to sail between the enemy ships and not to fire until they could rake them. This was dangerous, because it meant they had to take the French broadsides as they came up. However, their raking fire did terrible damage. Even more important, the ships that broke through were behind the enemy and stopped them escaping.

Nelson's plan worked, but the British did not win easily. One of the heroes of the battle was a little man only 4′ 10″ tall. He was Jean Lucas, captain of the French ship *Redoutable*. His ship engaged Nelson's *Victory*. They fired broadsides at each other and then grappled. Lucas called out his boarding parties. He had trained them well, so they were good shots and experts at throwing grenades. These men swarmed into their

Nelson falls during the battle of Trafalgar

rigging and swept *Victory*'s decks with musket fire. They also threw some 200 grenades into her. The English sailors fled below, and the French began to board. Just then, though, the *Temeraire* came to the rescue, pouring one broadside after another into the *Redoutable*. Lucas fought on, but now he had two enemies. Soon all of his guns were out of action, 500 of his crew of 640 were killed or wounded, and his ship was sinking. Only then, did he surrender.

During the attack on *Victory*, a French musketeer shot Nelson. The bullet smashed through his chest and broke his backbone. He died three hours later, but not before he had learnt that the battle was won. The French and Spaniards lost 4,400 dead, 2,500 wounded, 20,000 prisoners, and twenty ships out of their thirty-four. The British lost 450 killed, 1,200 wounded and no ships at all. Napoleon gave up all hope of invading Britain.

4 Wellington's Army

In 1807, the French invaded Spain and Portugal. The following year, the Duke of Wellington took a British army to help those countries defend themselves. We will visit his camp to talk to some of his soldiers.

First of all we meet Bob, a man from the artillery, who takes us to see his gun. The gun barrel is just like the ones we saw on Nelson's *Victory*. The carriage, though, has large wheels which make it easier to move on land. 'This is a field piece,' explains Bob. 'That means we can use it in battle. It's quite light, you see. For a siege we would want a much heavier gun – a twenty-four pounder, at least.' *'What ammunition do you use?'* Bob picks up a cannon ball that weighs about six pounds. 'At long range we use this round shot. If the ground is at all hard, it will bounce along like a marble, and kill quite a lot of men. Sometimes we use shells. A shell is filled with gunpowder, and has a fuse.' *'How do you light the fuse?'* 'The blast from the gun does that. If we time it right, the shell will burst over the heads of the enemy. One of their shells fell near me once. It lay on the ground, fizzing away. I just had time to dive into a hole before it exploded.' *'What are these cans?'* 'That's case shot. The canister is full of odd scraps of iron that fly through the air like a handful of loose stones. We can do terrible damage to the enemy with case, but only at short range.'

the Duke of Wellington

Next, we meet a cavalry officer, called Charles. He is a proud young man with black, curling moustaches. His horse is a handsome grey charger. 'The cavalry is the most important part of the army,' he says. 'One man in the cavalry is worth three in the infantry.' He draws his sabre to show us. It is curved for slashing, and is as sharp as a razor. 'One blow with that, and I can take off a man's head,' he boasts. 'My most important weapon, though, is my horse. If I came charging at you on Betsy here, I don't think you would stay

to argue.' *'When did you learn to ride?'* 'Almost before I could walk. My father has an estate in Leicestershire, which is grand hunting country. Just now, I chase Frenchmen instead of foxes. It is much more exciting. We go out scouting most days, often very near the enemy. Our horses are so good that the French gave up trying to catch us long ago.'

The last man we meet is a sergeant in the infantry, called William. 'This is my Brown Bess,' he explains, picking up a musket. He shows us how to load it by ramming a cartridge down the barrel. The cartridge is a tube of paper, with gunpowder and a musket ball inside. *'That takes a long time, William.'* 'Not at all. We can load and fire four times a minute, which is four times as fast as the French.' *'How far will your musket shoot?'* 'About three hundred yards, but we don't open fire above one hundred yards. At that range we usually hit someone, even if it's not the man we aim at.' *'The cavalry don't seem to think much of the infantry.'* 'They are a conceited lot. They are all right for scouting or chasing the enemy when he is defeated, but they aren't much use in a battle. Their trouble is that they think the war is one big hunting party. I overheard "Nosey"* himself complaining about them the other day. It seems Major-General Slade had been soundly beaten by a French force no bigger than his own. "They gallop at everything," he

* The soldiers' name for Wellington.

was saying, "so they fall straight into any trap the French may set for them."' *'Surely you infantry can't stop a cavalry charge.'*

For his answer, William draws his bayonet and clips it on his musket. He then thrusts it towards us. 'You imagine our battalion, eight hundred of us three ranks deep, standing so, in a square. There is no horse born that will jump a hedge like that. I have been fighting in the Peninsula for five years now, and I haven't seen French cavalry break a British square yet. What's more, I haven't seen our cavalry break a French square, either.'

115

5 A Day with Wellington's Army

It is the summer of 1813. Wellington has led his army into the heart of Spain. He has won a great victory, the Battle of Vitoria, and now the French are retreating to their own country. We will spend a day with the British army, which is moving after them.

At 5.00 in the morning the bugles sound, and the soldiers wake up, grumbling and cursing. In the half light, they take up their muskets and haversacks, and form ranks three ranks deep, ready to march. First, a body of light cavalry canter away. Next comes a detachment of light infantry in smart, dark-green uniforms. Almost at once, we hear the rumble of wheels, and a dozen light guns roll past, the horses drawing them at a quick trot. These three groups make up the advance guard. They have a busy time ahead of them and it will be exciting, too, if they meet any French.

Now comes the main army, moving much more slowly. Heavy cavalry lead, their steel helmets shining. Long columns of infantry tramp by, raising clouds of dust. Next come the supplies. There are herds of bullocks, for live meat travels easier than dead; there are strings of mules, laden with baggage; there are clumsy Spanish carts, whose wheels make a squeak like a knife edge being drawn over a plate. The men in charge of them are colourful, but villainous-looking Spaniards.

The road is already churned into ruts, but now the heavy guns appear. They are twenty-four pounders, for use in sieges. Long teams of straining oxen draw them, and we wonder how they manage in the mountains. More infantry follow. These are Portuguese, but they are as well disciplined as the British soldiers we saw earlier. From time to time we see little groups of women, for one soldier in twenty is allowed to bring his wife. An officer's wife goes past, riding a donkey, and carrying a pink parasol. A servant, on a mule, is nursing her baby, and tied behind the mule is a tired, unwilling goat. A body of cavalry brings up the rear. It is several miles from the head of the column.

A Day with Wellington's Army

The troops march for half an hour, then the bugles sound and they fall out for breakfast. This is a large, dry biscuit, and a piece of cold beef. Fifteen minutes later they are off again. They now march for an hour, rest for five minutes, and keep going like that until the midday break. They have more biscuits and beef, and rest through the worst of the heat. Then the march begins once more. With his musket and haversack, each man carries a load of sixty pounds. Their faces are caked with dust, save where trickles of perspiration wash it away. They are used to the discomfort, though, and keep up their spirits, laughing and joking. At last, the bugles sound a halt. The day's march is over. They have covered twelve miles at an average speed of two miles an hour.

The Quarter Master has chosen a good place to stay the night. The ground is flat, there is a stream, and there are trees nearby. Soon the men are busy making themselves comfortable. Some go to fetch water, some to collect wood, and others to draw rations – biscuits and beef again, but this time, a little rum as well.

We join a group who have lit a fire to brew tea. *'That was a hard day's march!'* we say. 'About average. We can cover thirty miles in a day, if we need to,' replies one of the soldiers. 'The worst march we ever did was the retreat from Madrid, last year,' says another. 'It was winter time you see, and usually we are snug in our billets at that time of year. The rain poured down and sometimes the mud was up to our knees. We had no tents, either, so we had to lie in the mud to sleep. What's more, the officer in charge of the supplies had sent them by another road. He made sure the French didn't eat our food, but neither did we. All we had for three days was acorns. Several of my friends died on that march.'

The men finish their supper, and lie down for the night. A few, fresh from England, twist and turn, but not the others. A mule starts braying, then another, and another, until dozens of them are making a hideous noise. The men sleep soundly until early morning when, at the first notes of the bugle, they are on their feet at once.

6 Napoleon in Russia

In 1811, Napoleon quarrelled with the Russians. Their ruler, Tsar Alexander I, had refused his offer of friendship, they were threatening his friends the Poles, and they insisted on trading with Britain against his will. Napoleon decided to invade Russia. He gathered a force of over half a million men. They came from twenty nations, including Italy, Poland, Germany, Holland and Switzerland. Only one-third was French. You will remember that Napoleon had 300,000 troops fighting in Spain.

As Napoleon advanced, the Russian armies fell back. They drove away the cattle, destroyed the crops and burnt the villages. The country is an enormous, grassy plain, and Napoleon's men began to think they were going to march for ever through vast, empty spaces. Napoleon was making for Moscow. The capital was St. Petersburg, but Moscow was larger, and was in the heart of Russia. The Tsar ordered his army to save it. Their commander was General Kutuzov. He had lost an eye in a battle with the Turks, he was so fat that he could not ride a horse, and he was 68 years old. For all that, he was an excellent soldier. He decided to make a stand at Borodino, a village 70 miles from Moscow.

When he realized the Russians were going to fight, Napoleon was delighted. He was not so pleased, though, when he saw where they were. Kutuzov had chosen a piece of country broken up with ravines and woods. They made it impossible for Napoleon to manoeuvre his men, using the clever tactics that had helped him win other battles. Also, the Russians had had time to build themselves trenches, and protect their artillery with mounds of turf.

Each side had about 600 guns, so the battle opened with the roaring of well over a thousand cannon. Napoleon had a plan, but it did not work. All he could rely on was the courage of his troops. They attacked the Russian positions again and again until, in places, the dead lay eight deep on the ground. The Russians fought like tigers. They were used to doing battle with the Turks, who always tortured and killed their prisoners. Russian soldiers never surrendered, but went on fighting to the end. Napoleon's army was the better, though, so they took the Russian positions one by one. General Kutuzov decided to retreat. He led away two-thirds of his army, having lost 44,000

men. Napoleon could not pursue him, for he had lost 33,000 himself. Dead and wounded lay everywhere. The senior surgeon in the French army sawed off 200 shattered limbs during the day, and his assistants were just as busy. However, the road to Moscow lay open.

Though Napoleon entered Moscow in triumph a few days later, he was soon a disappointed man. He had expected wealthy citizens to come and greet him, but they had left. All that remained were criminals and beggars. Next, soon after the French arrived, the Russians set fire to the city. They had taken away their fire engines, so four-fifths of it was destroyed. Worst of all, though, the Tsar showed no signs of wanting peace. Napoleon sent him several messages, but he just ignored them. In the end, Napoleon saw it was hopeless: he decided to leave Russia. He had wasted valuable time, though. The first snows fell as the French left the blackened ruins of Moscow, and soon their army was in the grip of a terrible winter.

the battle of Borodino

Men struggled through blizzards, their faces frost-bitten. Any that fell behind were killed by Cossack cavalry. The most difficult problem was to find food for the horses. One soldier kept his alive by creeping into the Russian camp, and stealing their hay. Few horses were as lucky, though. Most of them died, and later, so did the men. Only a few thousand staggered home. One of the last to arrive was a giant of a man, all in tatters. He was one of Napoleon's most famous generals, Marshal Ney, but some sentries who stopped him did not recognise him. 'Who are you?' they asked.

Ney replied, 'I am the rearguard of the Grand Army.'

After a while, Napoleon had abandoned his soldiers, and raced on in a sleigh. Back in France, he raised more troops. He fought on for another two years, but his old enemies, Prussia and Austria, had taken heart and joined the Russians. Meanwhile, Wellington was invading the South of France along with the Spaniards and Portuguese. In 1814, the Prussians under General Blücher captured Paris, and Napoleon surrendered.

7 The Battle of Waterloo

In 1814, after Napoleon had been defeated, he was given the little island of Elba in the Mediterranean to rule. This was generous treatment from his enemies, but in 1815 he decided to return to France. By then a brother of the King who had been guillotined was on the throne. He was Louis XVIII. Louis ordered soldiers to arrest Napoleon. When he saw them, Napoleon stepped forward and opened his greatcoat to expose his chest. 'I am your Emperor,' he said, 'kill me if you like.' 'Shoot him,' ordered the officers, but the men cheered Napoleon and ran to join him. Soon all his old soldiers were with him— the ones that were still alive— and Louis XVIII fled.

Napoleon was still in great danger, though, because there were powerful armies all round France, including the British and the Prussians who were in Belgium. He started by attacking the Prussians who were under Blücher at Ligny. He defeated them, but most of them escaped, and Blücher managed to hold them together. Two days later, Napoleon met the British at Waterloo, just south of Brussels. It was to be the first time he ever fought them. 'It will be a picnic,' he told one of his generals who warned him to be careful.

To the joy of the English soldiers, Wellington had been put in charge. 'Nosey has got the command,' said one of them. 'Won't we give them a beating now!' Wellington, though, was far from happy. Nearly all his best soldiers had been sent to fight in America, and

the ones he had were raw recruits who had never been in battle.

All Wellington could do was to stay on the defensive and hope that Blücher would come and help him. He put most of his men behind the brow of a hill, so that the enemy gunners could not see them, and sent some of his troops forward into some farmhouses, which they hurriedly fortified. He hoped they might break up the French attack before it advanced too far. Wellington kept his nerve, though. At the worst moment in the battle he was carefully studying the French army through his telescope, while his second in command, the Marquis of Anglesey, was sitting on his horse beside him. Suddenly, a cannon ball struck the Marquis, who yelled to Wellington, 'By God, Sir, I have lost my leg.' Wellington looked at the shattered, bleeding limb. 'By God, Sir, so you have,' he said, and turned back to his telescope.

Napoleon, on the other hand, was not at his best. He had piles, so it was painful for him to sit on his horse. At one point his officers were astonished to see him waddle off behind some bushes with his legs wide apart. He had gone to change his bandages.

The battle began with a splendid attack by some French infantry, and it might have succeeded had not the English cavalry charged and scattered them. Unfortunately, the English horsemen, who did a lot of hunting at home, chased the fugitives as if they were foxes. They rode much too close to the main French army, where they stuck in the mud and many of them were killed.

The French came back to the attack, captured one of the farmhouses, and pressed on to the main British army. The fighting was now so fierce, and men were falling so fast that one English officer wondered if everyone was going to be killed on both sides.

Most of the attacks came from French cavalry. The English infantry formed squares. The men fresh from England were terrified, but they soon saw that if they stood firm the horsemen could not ride into them. Napoleon thought, though, that if he made a really determined effort, the battle was his. He turned to his best soldiers, the cavalry of the Imperial Guard, and said, 'Follow me!' He led them to the weakest point in the British line, then, standing aside, ordered them to attack. They made a magnificent charge, but they could not break the British squares. Volley after

the French capture the farmhouse

a British square under attack

volley crashed into them so that the ground was heaped with dead and wounded. The survivors fled. A cry of dismay went up from the French, 'The Guard is retreating!'

Then, at last, the Prussians began to arrive. Blücher had promised Wellington he would join him early in the morning, but his first men did not appear until four in the afternoon. It was almost too late, but not quite. The Prussians wanted revenge for the Battle of Ligny, and the sight of this new enemy was too much for the weary French. Soon the whole of Napoleon's army was in full flight.

Some days later, Napoleon surrendered to the British, who sent him as a prisoner to the little island of St. Helena, in the middle of the Atlantic. There he died in 1821. Wellington went back to England in triumph, but he did not boast about his victory. When someone asked him what he thought of Waterloo, all he said was, 'It was a damned close-run thing.'

the Old Guard retreat

The Battle of Waterloo

Napoleon leaves the battlefield

Work Section

Understand Your Work

1 France Under Napoleon
1 Where does Monsieur Lebois live? Give the town and the street.
2 What was the Estates-General? Why did Louis XVI call it?
3 What did Monsieur Lebois hope would happen when the Estates-General met?
4 Why was he disappointed?
5 What building did the Paris mob destroy? What people were executed? How was this done?
6 On what countries did the Jacobins make war?
7 What was Napoleon before he became Emperor?
8 What did Napoleon do for France as a whole? (Don't forget the religious changes.)
9 What improvements did Napoleon make in Paris?
10 With what countries was Napoleon at war in 1812?

2 The British Navy
1 What prevented the French from invading Britain?
2 How were the guns of a battleship arranged?
3 What were 'firing a broadside' and 'raking an enemy'?
4 What was a midshipman?
5 Describe the work and duties of a midshipman.
6 List the stages in firing a gun.
7 Why did the French fire at their enemies' rigging? Where did the British fire?
8 How were men made to join the Navy?
9 In what ways was life at sea unpleasant?
10 Why was there a mutiny in 1797? What happened as a result?

3 The Battle of Trafalgar
1 Where was the French navy in 1803? Why was this inconvenient for Napoleon?
2 What plans did Napoleon make for the invasion of Britain?
3 Describe Villeneuve's movements until he reached Cadiz.
4 What was Nelson doing in the meantime?
5 What plans did Villeneuve make before the Battle of Trafalgar?
6 What did Nelson do with the half of the fleet that he led into battle? What did Collingwood do with the other half?
7 Why were the French ships unable to escape?
8 Which French ship attacked the *Victory*? Why did the attack fail?
9 What happened to Nelson?
10 Draw up a table to show the losses on both sides.

4 Wellington's Army
1 Why did the Duke of Wellington take a British army to Spain?
2 What was meant by saying a gun was a 'twenty-four pounder'? (Clue: Bob's gun was a six-pounder.)
3 Describe the three types of ammunition used by the artillery.
4 What weapon did a cavalryman carry?
5 What was a more important weapon for him?
6 What did the infantry soldier call his musket?
7 How did he load it?
8 How many shots could he fire in a minute?
9 At what range did he open fire?
10 How did infantry stop a cavalry charge?

5 A Day with Wellington's Army
1 What battle did Wellington win in 1813? What did the French do afterwards?
2 What troops were in the advance guard of Wellington's army?
3 Name three ways in which supplies travelled.
4 What foreign soldiers were there in Wellington's army?
5 What women were with the army?
6 For how long did the army march at a time?
7 How far did the army march in a day, on average? How far could it march, if required?
8 What food did the men have?
9 What did the Quarter-Master look for when choosing a camp site?
10 Describe the discomforts of marching in Spain a) in summer b) in winter.

6 Napoleon in Russia
1 Why did Napoleon make war on Russia?
2 Why did he take so many foreigners in his army?
3 What did the Russian armies do at first?
4 Why did the Russians decide to fight a battle?
5 What position did Kutuzov choose?
6 Why did Napoleon find it difficult to defeat the Russians?
7 What happened to Moscow after the French arrived?
8 Why did Napoleon decide to leave Russia?
9 What happened to most of his army on the way home?
10 What enemies did Napoleon have to face on his return? When did he surrender?

7 The Battle of Waterloo
1 Where was Napoleon sent in 1814?
2 When did he decide to return to France?
3 What victory did he win?
4 Why was Wellington afraid Napoleon might beat him? What plans did he make for the Battle of Waterloo?
5 What did the English cavalry do, at the start of the battle?
6 How did the English infantry fight off the French cavalry?
7 What happened to the Imperial Guard?
8 How did the battle end?
9 What happened to Napoleon, after Waterloo?
10 What was Wellington's opinion of the battle?

Use Your Imagination

1 Imagine you are Napoleon just after he has come to power. Write a list of instructions for your ministers, saying what changes you want made in France. (1)
2 Write a letter Madame Lebois might have sent to her son. (1)
3 Write a story about a sailor who was pressganged into the Navy. (2)
4 You are one of the mutineers of 1797. Write a letter to the government, asking them to improve conditions in the Navy. (2)
5 Nelson gathers his captains together to explain his plans for the Battle of Trafalgar. Write what he says. (3)
6 You are a French sailor on the *Redoutable*. Give a running commentary on the Battle of Trafalgar as you see it. (3)
7 A cavalryman and an infantryman have an argument about which is the more important for the army. Write what they say. (4)
8 You are the Commissary, that is, the officer in charge of the supplies in Wellington's army. Write a list of the things you order from time to time. (4, 5)
9 You have just joined Wellington's army as a soldier in the infantry. Write a letter home, describing your life. (4, 5)
10 You are in charge of the advance guard. Write Wellington a report of an encounter with some French soldiers. (4, 5)
11 You are one of Napoleon's soldiers who has returned from Russia. Write a conversation you have with your family. (6)
12 Say what you think might have happened if the French had won the Battle of Trafalgar. (5, 6)
13 You are a French soldier at Waterloo. Give a running commentary on the battle, as you see it. (7)
14 Suppose you could go back in time, and talk to Napoleon after his coronation in 1804. What advice would you give him? (2–7)
15 A Frenchman and an Englishman have an argument. The Frenchman thinks Napoleon was a great man, the Englishman disagrees. Write what they say. (All)

Further Work

1 Read more about a) King Louis XVI of France and his Queen, Marie Antoinette b) the Reign of Terror under the Jacobins, including the troubles in La Vendée c) Napoleon's early life.
2 Find pictures of buildings put up in Paris in Napoleon's time.
3 Madame Lebois mentions Napoleon's 'new Empress' (p. 107). Find out who she was. Who was Empress before her? Read the story of her life.
4 Read about Napoleon's campaign in Egypt, and Nelson's victory at the Battle of the Nile.
5 Read the full story of the naval mutinies of 1797.
6 Find and copy plans or diagrams of Nelson's *Victory*.
7 Read more about the war in Spain, especially the campaign of 1812 and Wellington's victory at Salamanca.
8 What is the name of your local regiment? Find out if it fought with Wellington in Spain, or at Waterloo.
9 Read about some of Napoleon's victories not mentioned here, e.g. Rivoli and Austerlitz.
10 There are many novels about the French Revolution and the Napoleonic Wars. Find and read some of them. Your English teacher or your librarian will help you choose suitable books.

The Publisher would like to thank the following for
permission to reproduce photographs:

Bolton Metropolitan Borough Arts Department, p. 34; City of
Bristol Museum and Art Gallery, p. 62; Cooper-Bridgeman
Library, p. 27, p. 53 and p. 102; Darlington Museum, p. 53;
Mary Evans Picture Library, p. 32, p. 71, p. 90 and p. 121;
Richard Green Galleries, p. 14 and p. 47; Institute of
Agriculture and Economics, Oxford, p. 11; Mansell Collection,
p. 38; Musée Carnavalet, Paris, p. 107 (top); Musée du Louvre,
p. 107 (bottom); National Army Museum, p. 97 (top and
bottom), p. 103 (top and bottom), and p. 123 (bottom);
National Gallery of Canada, Ottowa, pp. 98–9; National
Maritime Museum, p. 58, p. 60, p. 63, p. 109, p. 111 and
p. 113 (bottom); National Portrait Gallery, p. 46 (right) and
p. 62; Peter Newark's Western Americana, p. 32, p. 95 and
p. 101; Northumberland County Council, p. 52; Radio Times
Hulton Picture Library, p. 56 and p. 63 (left); Science Museum,
p. 33, p. 34, p. 37, p. 46, p. 56, p. 57 and p. 59; Sotheby's,
Belgravia, p. 11 (bottom); Tate Gallery, p. 113 (top); Victoria
and Albert Museum, p. 33 (bottom), p. 114, p. 122 and p. 123;
Walker Art Gallery, Liverpool, p. 21 and pp. 124–5;
Waterways Museum, p. 50.

Illustrations by Victor Ambrus, Robert Ayton, Dick Barnard,
Oliver Frey, Roger Gorringe, Richard Hook, Malcolm
McGregor, Christine Molan, Tony Morris and Maurice Wilson.

Cover illustration by Christine Molan